SAMUEL TAYLOR COLERIDGE

Born at Ottery St Mary, Devonshire, in 1772 and educated at Christ's Hospital and Jesus College, Cambridge. Settled near Wordsworth at Nether Stowey in Somerset in 1797 and issued *Lyrical Ballads* with him in 1798. Visited Germany, 1798–9, settled at Keswick in 1800, worked in Malta and travelled in Italy, 1804–6. In 1816 went to live with the Gillmans at Highgate, where he became the centre of a wide circle of acquaintances until his death in 1834.

Samuel Taylor Coleridge
On the Constitution of the CHURCH and STATE According to the Idea of Each

Edited, with an introduction, by
JOHN BARRELL
Lecturer in English, University of Cambridge

320.941

J. M. Dent & Sons Ltd, London

Contents

A Note on this Edition

The first edition of *Church and State* appeared in 1830. A second was called for in the same year, and a third came out in 1839, edited by H. N. Coleridge, who supplied a few footnotes mainly to do with legal issues; the version of *Church and State* in Shedd's *Collected Works* of Coleridge, published in America, is more or less a reprint of the third edition. The first part of the first edition was untidily split up into paragraphs, and before the book was reprinted Coleridge improved this arrangement by dividing this first part into chapters, and by adding a few paragraphs of clarification here and there. H. N. Coleridge claimed to have produced his edition from 'the author's corrected copies', but as almost all his changes are stylistic, and such as Coleridge can hardly have authorized, it is the second edition that is here reprinted. I have, however, adopted most of H. N. Coleridge's emendations (though not his accentuation) of Coleridge's Greek phrases and quotations, which were horribly mangled by the typesetter in the first two editions.

This is the first edition of *Church and State* to be annotated at all fully, and as such it can hardly hope to be in any way complete. I have explained such contemporary references as seemed to require a note, and have done my best to trace Coleridge's quotations to their sources; but Coleridge almost invariably, and often deliberately, misquotes, and for reasons of space I have not always pointed out how he diverges from his originals. The three main editions have been collated, but the only changes from edition to edition that have been noted are those which seem to me to involve significant changes in Coleridge's meaning. I have not attempted to point out the numerous similarities between passages in *Church and State* and in Coleridge's earlier works. I am grateful to Miss Mary Bonner, Herbie Butterfield, Leon Burnett and Miss Jania Miller for the help they have given me in producing this edition.

Abbreviations

The following abbreviations are used in the notes:

AR   *Aids to Reflection*, 1825 edition.

BL   *Biographia Literaria*, Everyman edition, ed. Watson.

F   *The Friend*, ed. Rooke, Part IV (two vols.), 1969, of the Bollingen Foundation *Collected Works of S.T. Coleridge*.

H.N.C. Henry Nelson Coleridge, editor of the third edition of *Church and State*.

[The notes are placed at the end of each chapter or section so as to distinguish them from Coleridge's own footnotes, which are designated by typographical symbols.]

Introduction

On the Constitution of the Church and State was the last book by Coleridge to be published during his lifetime, and one in which almost all his various interests—in political theory, theology, education and historiography—are brought together. It is, with Burke's *Reflections on the Revolution in France*, one of the few classic works of conservative thought in English, and one which unites two remarkable traditions of political theory: that of Hooker and such early seventeenth-century eulogists of English Common Law as Sir Edward Coke and Sir John Davies, and that of the Romantic conservatism of Herder and his followers in Germany. The main part of *Church and State* is an enquiry into the nature and history of the English Constitution; and the historical technique used in this enquiry—and characterized by John Stuart Mill when he said that Coleridge asks of every institution, 'What is the meaning of it?'—was extremely influential on English historical thought in the decades after the book's publication. It is in *Church and State*, also, that we find Coleridge's fullest statement of the need for a 'clerisy', a body of teachers endowed by the nation and disseminated throughout the country; Coleridge's ideas on education were the beginning of an alternative tradition in the popular education movement, opposed to the vocational and science-based schemes of the Utilitarians, and in this respect *Church and State* was particularly influential on the educationalists within the Broad Church movement.

The book appeared in 1830, four years before Coleridge's death. By that time he had moved from his early, intense support of the French Revolution to a version of conservative constitutionalism, without, he claimed, ever changing the bases of his political beliefs. The book was written, in the first place, in response to one of the several Catholic Emancipation Bills introduced in the 1820s, which proposed to open the Houses of Parliament to Roman Catholics. Coleridge was anxious to support the granting of Catholic Relief, but only if it were accompanied by securities to protect the institutions which are the subject of this book from any attempt by Rome to establish a political base in England. In fact an Emancipation Act was passed in 1829, and this perhaps robbed *Church and State* of some of its point; Coleridge's doubts about the measure were largely satisfied by the Act in its final form, and one can detect an embarrassment on his part at not having more to say about it. But although it is true that the main interest of the book does not depend on its relevance to immediate political issues, it is still full of Coleridge's awareness and apprehension of two important, and related, historical movements: the agitation for parliamentary reform (the Reform Act followed in 1832), and the increasing influence of rationalist and empirical philosophy, in particular of Utilitarianism, on the minds of the educated.

It will be clear from this that *On the Constitution of the Church and State* is a work of that tradition of Romantic conservatism which emerged as a reaction to the ideals of the Enlightenment, particularly of the French and the Scottish Enlightenments, and which understood history not as progressive and linear, but as a process of growth and decay. For the philosophers of this tradition, 'God is the unity of every nation'; and so for them political theory began with the study of a society as a whole, as an organism, and not, as it had begun in France, with the individual, unqualified by and abstracted from that conspiration of local and national influences 'without which or divided from which', in Coleridge's phrase, 'his Being cannot even be thought'. And with this insistence came another, that the institutions of a nation were to be judged not by the degree to which they conformed with abstract notions of the useful and the rational, but in terms of their appropriateness to, and their meaning within, the national culture of which they were a part.

But there are a number of factors that make Coleridge's conservatism different from that of the Germans from whom he had learned. He took from Herder, for example, the notion that a nation's institutions must be understood in terms of the needs of a national culture; but he was too much of a Tory to be a convinced cultural relativist, and went on to argue that, by the coming together of a number of fortunate historical accidents, the legal and political institutions of England had developed a quite exceptional degree of sympathy with the needs of the English people. For this emphasis Coleridge was indebted to Burke, of course, but perhaps more to his reading in the English seventeenth century: in his first chapter he quotes, or rather adapts, a magnificent passage from Sir John Davies on the 'connaturalness' of English Law with the genius of the English people; and in a volume of Hooker, against the famous statement, 'A Law is the Deed of the whole Body Politick, whereof if ye judge your selves to be any part, then is the Law even your Deed also', Coleridge made a long marginal note in which he interpreted this as having particular force in relation to the Customary Law of England.

Among the fortunate accidents of history were the facts that, since 1066, England had not been invaded, and had thus 'the insular privilege of a self-evolving constitution', and that, by the establishment of the Anglican Church, she had been spared the influence of Rome, and had developed a truly national church as well as national political institutions. Coleridge tries hard to distinguish this view of history from that parody of Burke's philosophy which argued that England in 1830 was at a peak of cultural maturity, and that to interfere with her system of government would be sacrilege—although the threat of Reform sometimes pushes him, as we shall see, towards that position. But Coleridge more usually thinks of England as a nation already in decline, from a peak in Elizabeth's reign or in the Commonwealth; the point of his argument is that the process of decay could be halted not by overthrowing her institutions, or by chipping away at them, but by trying to see what it was in them that had once been valuable, and whether they could, once again, realize the 'ideas' for which they existed.

Coleridge differs from his German contemporaries in this too, that whereas an idealist and Romantic conservatism had become the dominant philosophy in early nineteenth-century, pre-industrial Germany, in England Coleridge defended the philosophy in what seemed to him a uniformly hostile political and intellectual climate. There was no lack of politicians in England who agreed with Coleridge on various matters of practical policy; but he found little value in that sort of agreement that was not based on an understanding of the principles of English political history, of the 'ideas' of Church and State. And whereas for German philosophers of history the empiricism and materialism of the Enlightenment were the products of an alien culture, whose imposition on the states of Germany they wrote to oppose, it seemed to Coleridge that a native strain of the 'mechanico-corpuscular' philosophy, from Locke through to Paley and to Bentham, had become the dominant influence on English cultural life, justifying a blind pragmatism in politics and the brutalities of the industrial system. For him the history of England since 1688 had been a 'misgrowth', which had separated the ruling and the intellectual classes from the people; and he understood this as the result especially of economic change in the eighteenth century: 'the main Pillar of Mr Locke's reputation' arose, he argued,

from the enormous commerce of the Nation, & the enormous increase of Number in the Profession of the Law consequent hence, and 2. from the small number of the Universities & the nature of the Tutorships & Professorships in them, & 3 & principally from the circumstance that the preferment of the Clergy in general is wholly independent of their Learning or their Talents, but does depend very greatly on a certain passive obedience of Satellites to the Articles of the Church. . . .*

For Coleridge, the people alone still understood intuitively the nature and the ends of political organization, an intuition that

* See *Coleridge on the Seventeenth Century*, ed. Brinkley (1955), p. 90.

was being obscured for them, too, by the wrong sort of education or the lack of it, and by an economic system which converted them into means, into 'engines for the manufactory of new rich men', and did not include them in the ends of industrial progress. Coleridge felt the power of the 'misgrowth' in English history the more sharply, because he had himself been a 'necessitarian', a follower of Locke and of Hartley, before his reading in English seventeenth-century platonism, and German idealism, led him out of the deterministic universe in which he had spent the last years of the eighteenth century. *On the Constitution of the Church and State* is the final statement of his emancipation from the tradition of English empiricism.

Coleridge begins his argument by explaining the meaning of the word 'idea' in his title. An idea, he says, is

that conception of a thing, which is not abstracted from any particular state, form, or mode, in which the thing may happen to exist at this or at that time; nor yet generalized from any number or succession of such forms or modes; but which is given by the knowledge of *its ultimate aim.*

He makes his meaning clearer still by explaining the difference between an idea and a 'conception'. A conception, he says, is a conscious act of the understanding. When we bring 'any given object or impression into the same class with any number of other objects, or impressions, by means of some character or characters common to them all'; when, in short, we generalize about the objects of our experience, then the proper name for our generalization is a 'conception'. And because it is a generalization, a conception is something which occurs, in order of thought, *after* we have become aware of the objects to which the generalization applies. An idea, on the other hand, is not grasped by the understanding, but by the higher, intuitive faculty of reason; it necessarily *precedes* the objects of which it is the idea, and may be said, indeed, to produce them. Thus, the idea men have of what a society is may be said to produce a society; and thus also the constitution of a state is produced, and its growth is determined, by the idea of what a constitution ought to be.

An idea, says Coleridge, 'may very well exist, aye, and powerfully influence a man's thoughts and actions, without his being distinctly conscious of the same, much more without his being competent to express it in definite words'. It is the privilege of a very few to be actively conscious of the existence of ideas, but that this is so does not make their existence any less certain. The history of the English Constitution, says Coleridge,

demonstrates the continued influence of such an idea, or ultimate aim, on the minds of our fore-fathers, in their characters and functions as public men; alike in what they resisted and in what they claimed; in the institutions and forms of polity which they established, and with regard to those, against which they more or less successfully contended . . . [so that] we speak, and have a right to speak, of the idea itself, as actually existing, *i.e.*, as a *principle*, existing in the only way in which a principle can exist—in the minds and consciences of the persons, whose duties it prescribes, and whose rights it determines.

The constitution, the state, the nation, are thus all understood as essentially psychological phenomena; they exist, not as a set of institutions, as a body of laws, as a social structure or whatever, but as 'ideas'; 'the State', wrote Coleridge in one of his notebooks, 'is actual only in the Idea. The Idea is the Reality of the State, yea, *is* the State.' In advancing this position, Coleridge was much indebted to Burke, and except that the discussion of the state was, for Coleridge, a problem as much of metaphysics as of political theory, he would not have claimed that this assertion of the psychological essence of the state marked any particular step forward in conservative thinking. For Burke, a nation was 'an idea of continuity', and a society 'a partnership not only between those who are living, but between those who are living, those who are dead, and those who are to be born'. We can see clearly in these descriptions the germ of Coleridge's idea: a 'partnership' implies an agreement between the dead, the living, and the unborn (the agreement which Paine found so absurd) about what a state should be; it implies that, although the particular circumstances of a state may change, the idea of the state, its essence, does not change, and will be equally apparent in the future as it has been in the past.

Burke's theory of the nation as 'an idea of continuity' was one arrived at mainly, of course, in response to the French Revolution, and to the sight of the constitution of France being violently overthrown, in deference, as Burke saw it, to an abstract and over-simple political doctrine. Coleridge shared this distrust of the rationalism of the *philosophes*—he dismissed such thinking as 'metapolitics'; but writing in 1829, nearly forty years after Burke, he was conscious as we have seen of a greater danger to a true understanding of the state—the increasing importance of the empirical social sciences, of the political economy of Smith, Bentham and Malthus, which substituted the 'guess-work of general consequences' for 'moral and political philosophy'. For Coleridge, the true aim of political philosophy was to grasp what he, in common with Hegel and others, called 'ideas'—the principles that governed the growth of human societies and of the universe. By ideas the past, present and future were bound within a coherent process, in which each movement, each transition, could be seen in terms of an ultimate aim. And under the influence of German idealism, the idea of the state Coleridge inherited from Burke became explicitly metaphysical—an idea was a part of the divine plan for the universe, which man could grasp only by his reason, that faculty in him which partook also of divinity.

After explaining what he means by an 'idea', Coleridge goes on to describe the idea of the state. The word 'state' has two meanings for him: a larger meaning in which 'it is equivalent to Realm and includes the Church', and another, narrower meaning, in which it is distinguished from the Church, and comes to mean the body of our political institutions. It is the idea of the state in this narrow sense that Coleridge first sets out to explore, by examining the idea of the constitution.

A constitution, he says, is the 'law of balance' between the two antagonistic forces of Permanence and Progression within a state. The interest of Permanence he sees as being upheld by the proprietors of land, and that of Progression by the members of the 'manufacturing, mercantile, distributive, and professional classes', which are characterized not by fixed but by moveable property; by money and by acquired skills, and not by land. In England, the organization of the Houses of Parliament was intended to preserve the law of balance between these two forces. The proprietors of land were divided into two classes, the 'Major and Minor Barons'. The Major Barons composed the House of Lords; the Minor Barons, 'too numerous, and yet individually too weak, to sit and maintain their rights in person', were to elect representatives to form a minority in the House of Commons—'the majority of which was formed by representatives chosen by the cities, ports, and boroughs'. Because the Minor Barons were liable, according to circumstances, to sympathize either with the Major Barons or with the burgesses, a balance was maintained within Parliament whereby the interest of Permanence was counterpoised by that of Progression, and the interests of the most powerful individuals of the state were counterpoised by those of the gentry and the burgesses sitting in the Lower House. The King is described (provisionally, for his role is discussed more fully later in the book) as the 'beam' of the constitutional scales.

The germ of one half of this idea of the nature of government is to be found in the 'law of balance' worked out by the seventeenth-century political theorist James Harrington, whom Coleridge greatly admired: 'as is the proportion or balance of dominion or property in land, such is the nature of the empire'. The other half derives from Burke, who had seen the two principles of 'conservation and correction' at work in the history of the English Constitution, and had insisted, although perhaps with small practical conviction, that 'a state without the means of some change is without the means of its conservation'. But, once again, the idea taken from Burke has been transmuted by the influence of Germany. The two forces identified by Coleridge, and which he sees as represented by the landed classes and by the bourgeoisie, are more than the interests represented by particular power-groups, and are indeed the two forces the existence of which is presupposed by any idea of change, of process, within the universe. They are analogous, for example, to the two 'ultimate concepts' recognized by Schiller, of Person and Condition, 'a something in man which endures and something which constantly changes'. These two antithetical concepts are synthesized, for Schiller, in Absolute Being, as for Coleridge the opposing forces of Permanence and Progession tend towards union in the Ideal State; so that Coleridge's idea of the state (in the narrow sense) is of a fixed relation which binds the two forces, one fixed, one always fluid. There is, in fact, a dialectical triad-in-embryo at work in Coleridge's argument, disguised by his use of the traditional vocabulary of English constitutionalism, of scales and of balance, but quite apparent when read in the light of the German philosophers with whom he was more or less familiar.

This then is Coleridge's idea of the constitution of the state; how we view it depends on how far we are satisfied that it offers any genuine possibility of change. A number of critics have found the idea more rigidly conservative than Coleridge intended, as though he fell into the error of writing an apology for the unreformed English Parliament, under the pretence of revealing the idea of every constitution. There is a certain amount of justice in this view: Coleridge explicitly denies that his account of the organization of Parliament is an historical account—it is, he insists, a description of the *idea*—but nevertheless he appears at times to be describing the history of the English Constitution as a movement towards that ideal constitution that has now finally been realized in England; and when he does argue in this way he is of course substituting for the 'idea' of the constitution, an 'abstraction' from the English model. At one point he speaks of the 'final balance' that has been achieved between Permanence and Progression in our own constitution—the phrase does not suggest a state open to change; and we are entitled anyway to be suspicious of an idea of the state which decrees in advance what elements of progress are according to the idea, and which establishes an unchangeable relationship between the permanent and progressive interests within the state. Coleridge's preoccupation with the virtues of seventeenth-century 'balance' are sometimes at odds with his search for unity; at least, he does not always recognize that the two may not be the same. But whether or not his idea of the constitution was devised to shore up the tottering, unreformed Houses of Parliament, it was certainly an attempt to revive a tradition of political theory which would be an alternative to the prevailing mechanical and empiricist tradition, and which would see constitutional change not as the sudden replacement of one static political system with another, but as process, as growth.

What Coleridge has so far described is the idea of the constitution of the state, in the narrow sense of the word 'state', in which it is distinct from, and as it were in antithesis to, the church. He now sets out to describe the constitution of the state in the wider sense, that is, of the realm or nation. For the nation includes not only the interests of Permanence and Progression, but a third interest, which has to do with the cultural development of the people. This third interest Coleridge calls the 'National Church', and his idea of the National Church has been regarded by many as his most important contribution to political theory—certainly it is the only part of his theory remembered today.

Coleridge begins his account of the National Church (which is, as we shall see, not to be confused with the Christian Church) by discussing the nature of property. It was, he says,

common to all the primitive races, that in taking possession of a new country, and in the division of land into hereditable estates among the individual warriors or heads of families, a reserve should be made for the nation itself.

This reserve Coleridge calls the Nationalty, and it is, according to the idea of the state, one of the two constituent factors of the 'Commonwealth'. The other, the land in private hands, which Coleridge called the Propriety, was not 'so entirely a property as not to remain, to a certain extent, national'; it was placed by the nation in the trust of the landowners, and this trust imposed on them social duties. The Nationalty, on the other hand, was not so exclusively the nation's as not to admit of individual tenure; but the usufruct of the Nationalty could not be alienated from its original purpose, which was to support a body of men charged with looking after the moral and cultural interests of the nation. This body of men Coleridge named the 'clerisy'.

In arguing the importance of the National Church, Coleridge makes what has become a famous distinction between 'civilization' and 'cultivation'. The interests of both Permanence and Progression, he argues, depend for their survival on 'a continuing and progressive civilization';

but civilization in itself is but a mixed good, if not far more a corrupting influence, the hectic of disease, not the bloom of health, and a nation so distinguished more fitly to be called a varnished than a polished people; where this civilization is not grounded in *cultivation*, in the harmonious developement of those qualities and faculties that characterize our *humanity*. We must be men in order to be citizens.

This passage places the discussion of the 'clerisy' clearly in the context of early nineteenth-century England, and the book becomes, still more than it was before, a tract for the times as much as a work of formal political theory. And in the magnificent chapter, 'Regrets and Apprehensions', inserted in the middle of this discussion, Coleridge is eloquent in his conviction that a proper grasp of the idea of the National Church was especially necessary in his own period of rapid industrialization, in which 'those attainments, which give a man the power of doing what he wishes in order to obtain what he desires, are alone to be considered as knowledge, or admitted into the scheme of National Education'.

The Nationalty, then, was reserved to support a permanent class or order, the national clerisy, charged to superintend the cultivation of the nation. This order, the National Church, is not to be confused with the Christian Church, which has, by a 'blessed accident', become the usufructuary proprietor of the Nationalty, and which performs some, at least, of the duties of

xviii

a clerisy. The clerisy was originally understood to include, not merely theologians and divines, but the learned in all branches of knowledge. A small number of this order was to remain at universities, to 'cultivate and enlarge' existing knowledge, and to be the instructors of the rest of the order, who were to be distributed throughout the country, 'so as not to leave the smallest integral part or division without a resident guide, guardian, and instructor'. The task of this more numerous body, composed of schoolmasters as well as pastors or parsons, was

especially to diffuse through the whole community, and to every native entitled to its laws and rights, that quantity and quality of knowledge which was indispensable both for the understanding of those rights, and for the performance of the duties correspondent.

The Nationalty cannot be alienated from this original purpose without 'foul wrong' to the nation. It is a possession in which 'every free subject of the nation' has a living and permanent interest; it has been consecrated to 'the potential divinity in every man,

which is the ground and condition of his *civil* existence, that without which a man can be neither free nor obliged, and by which alone, therefore, he is capable of being a free subject—a citizen'.

This is a remarkable contribution to the theory of political obligation, and one quite crucial to Coleridge's argument: to alienate the Nationalty from its proper function is, he says, to release the people of a nation from their obligations to the state —being now, by the loss of their moral freedom consequent on their lack of cultivation, unfitted to discharge them.

It has seemed to some that the main purpose of the clerisy as Coleridge described it was to inculcate 'habits of docility' in the nation, and there is some small justice in this position. Thus if we see Coleridge's idea of the constitution as a means of confining the forces of progression within an essentially static idea of the state, then we are likely also to see the National Church as an institution teaching that static idea of the state as the only possible one; the clerisy has been compared by one sympathetic critic of Coleridge with the Russian Communist Party, I think with unconscious irony. Nor does Coleridge allow the possibility that the people educated by the clerisy might become sufficiently responsible to merit political representation, by virtue of their cultivation alone; he insists that the business of government is to do with the regulation of the Propriety and its protection, and that without a property-qualification no man can aspire to the franchise. The most he will concede is that it ought to be open to all members of society to obtain property, by their industry and talents.

This is, however, an excessively narrow view of the National Church, and one which ignores Coleridge's definition of cultivation as 'the harmonious developement of those qualities and faculties that characterize our *humanity*'. For Coleridge as for Hegel, a man's humanity is realized especially in the consciousness of his moral freedom, which enables him to give his assent to the contractual obligations imposed on him by society. We may well wonder by what means the majority of Englishmen in the 1820s were able to record this assent; but we should still recognize that to see the 'qualities that characterise our humanity' as finding their proper expression in the individual only as he is a free and consenting member of society, is not necessarily to undervalue the freedom of the individual. The charge of authoritarianism so repeatedly made against Hegel is easily evaded by Coleridge, for, as we have seen, there are circumstances—and ones not very unlike those he described as existing in the early nineteenth century—when for Coleridge a citizen could be 'neither free nor obliged'; if the National Church is not maintained and the citizens not educated, the state in the larger sense ceases to exist, for those who are not free members of a society cannot be obliged to it. And in this context we should remember also Coleridge's insistence that the state (in the narrow sense) has no jurisdiction over the Nationalty, which is the birthright of the nation as a whole, of those without political representation as well as of those with it. It has been argued that Coleridge's idea of the clerisy was interpreted in both these ways in the nineteenth century; and that while some readers of *Church and State* learned from it 'that the Church must take practical steps to realize the Kingdom of Heaven on earth',* others, more numerous, decided that 'the Church was most fitly employed in maintaining habits of sobriety, industry, and obedience in the lower orders'. It is worth pointing out, however, that while Coleridge was probably the first to advocate a programme of national education as 'cultivation' in any genuine sense, there were plenty of other, equally available authorities, whom Coleridge attacked energetically throughout his career, and whom the advocates of industry and obedience could with more justice have claimed as their teachers.

In his final chapter on the idea of the clerisy, Coleridge discusses 'what unfits, and what excludes from the National Church'. He argues that ministers of religion who owe allegiance to a 'foreign power' (he means the Pope), who are compelled to remain celibate, and who thus do not establish those bonds of kinship that would bind them to the interests of the nation, are to be excluded from the National Church, and may not be supported by the Nationalty. It is at this point that Coleridge's account of the 'insular privilege' of England's 'self-evolving' institutions comes closest to his more tentative discussion of Catholic Emancipation. The rest of the first part of the book is given over to the discussion of two outstanding questions, of which the first is the position of the king with respect to the state and to the National Church. The king, he argues, and the Houses of Parliament, as constituting the state in the narrow sense, have as the legitimate objects of their power 'all the interests and concerns of the Propriety, and rightfully those alone'. The king is, too, head of the National Church, 'the power of which in relation to its proper objects is rightfully exercised, according to the idea, by the King and the two Houses of Convocation [viz. of the Province of Canterbury], and by them alone'. The king is required by the Coronation Oath to protect the Nationalty from any attempt to subvert its

* See John Colmer, *Coleridge, Critic of Society* (1959), pp. 157–8.

xxi

safety and independence, and to refuse his consent to any measure which would prove thus subversive.

Finally in this first part Coleridge discusses 'the two *Conditions* of the health and vigour of a Body Politic'. The first of these is 'a due proportion of the free and permeative life and energy of the Nation to the organized powers brought within containing channels'. The organized powers are those which find expression in the institutions of the state, and in property to which the right of suffrage is attached; the free and permeative powers are extra-institutional, and characterized by the sort of property the ownership of which does not bring with it the right to vote. The tendency of the permeative powers to grow out of proportion to the organized powers is counteracted by their further tendency to become organized, as successful businessmen qualify for the electoral franchise.

It is convenient at this point to notice a confusion which appears here and elsewhere in Coleridge's argument, and which arises out of his attempt to reconcile the *idea* of the state with the actual distribution of power in England in 1830. Earlier in his argument he had justified the predominance of the Landed Interest in the House of Commons—a result partly of the survival of rotten boroughs—by saying that this increase in the representation of the interest of Permanence had been counteracted by the development of 'roads, canals, machinery, the press', by 'the might of public opinion'—in short by the 'free and permeative powers of the nation', which are, by implication, of the party of Progression. It is clear that Coleridge is trying to smuggle into his argument a new notion, that there should be a balance of Permanence and Progression not only in the state (in the narrow sense), but in the nation as a whole; and this new notion is obviously incompatible, at least in the industrial England that Coleridge describes, with that earlier one of the balance within Parliament, which now has to be thrown over. For if a balance of Permanence and Progression is to be maintained within Parliament, then in the nation as a whole the forces of Progression, whether organized or permeative, will predominate. But if this new sort of balance is to be achieved within the nation as a whole, it must be by a Parliament manifestly not ruled by the law of balance, and so not constituted 'according to the idea'. This part of the discussion, which must be intended as an argument against Reform, should instead have led Coleridge to support it; for by Reform sufficient of the permeative could have become organized powers to re-establish a due proportion of both in the Body Politic, and sufficient 'progressive' members could have been returned to re-establish the law of balance within the Houses of Parliament.

The second condition of the health of a Body Politic is 'a due proportion of the *potential* (latent, dormant) to the *actual* power'. The freedom of the English, Coleridge argues, has for centuries been based on the tacit understanding that the nation has delegated its power to Parliament, 'but not without measure and circumscription'; so that on the occasion of any gross departure from the idea of the constitution on the part of Parliament, the potential power of the nation manifests itself by 'the voice of the People which is the voice of God'; at such times the consent of the people is seen not as a passive thing, but as a matter of active moral will. The notion of 'potential power' has seemed to some critics to reveal a tendency in Coleridge's thought towards anarchy, which disturbs them; but Coleridge clearly intended it to be an answer to the advocates for Reform—that on the issues that genuinely concern them, the people have a voice—and to provide a security against that form of constitutional anarchy that Burke feared, whereby the state may be changed 'as much, and in as many ways, as there are floating fancies or fashions'.

This summary has taken us up to the end of the first part of *Church and State*, the part which contains most of what Coleridge had to say about educational and political theory. The remaining parts, except for the fine dialogue between an idealist and a man of this world, a sort of practical lesson in how an empirical may become an idealist philosopher, are shorter and of less interest to all except the ecclesiastical historian and perhaps the theologian. In the second section

Coleridge describes the idea of the Christian Church, as opposed to the National Church; he spends some time in the next section identifying, or rather re-identifying, for the job had been done often enough, the Pope with the Anti-Christ; and in the fourth (and apart from the Glossary and the Appendix, the final) section he comes round to revealing his objection to the Catholic Relief Act, that it did not make it sufficiently clear that ministers of the Catholic religion should not be kept by the Nationalty. There was no great likelihood that they would be, although Wellington's cabinet had discussed the issue a year or two before; it is a rather flat ending to a magnificent book.

In the middle decades of the nineteenth century no one doubted the importance of Coleridge's influence on political and educational thought in England: it was felt in Disraeli's Young England movement, in the Broad Church, and in the Christian Socialism of F. D. Maurice; for a while it 'humanized' the Utilitarianism of John Stuart Mill; Newman, Kingsley, Thomas and Matthew Arnold were all much indebted, directly or indirectly, to Coleridge's writings in general, and to *Church and State* in particular. To discuss the influence of the book within the compass of a brief introduction looks impossible; but if we combine the question of the influence of the book with that of the relevance of reprinting it today, the scope of our enquiry shrinks. Thus it is generally agreed that Coleridge had an influence on Disraeli, and it is true that in *Sybil*, for example, we find an admirable and properly Coleridgian concern with 'the culture of the popular sensibilities', as well as a Coleridgian disgust at the prospect of 'a Utopia of WEALTH and TOIL'. But the Conservative Party's lack of interest in the values implied by such phrases as these was hardly less apparent in the ministries of Disraeli than in those of his predecessors and successors; and as for any Coleridgian influence on conservative theory, we will look as hard in the Conservative Party of the last hundred years for any interest in political theory itself as for that. This is not, perhaps, Coleridge's fault; so that when one critic points out that 'no one has followed Coleridge in using the terms *Propriety* and *Nationalty* to differentiate between property which is privately held and that which is set aside for the nation',* the point is surely not that the distinction was not suggestive and challenging, but that it has been uncongenial to conservatives to assert it—especially since Coleridge's Propriety was not exclusively private property, but held in trust by landowners for the nation. The point is well made by Mill, in exactly this context: 'What says Sir Robert Inglis, or Sir Robert Peel . . . to such a doctrine as this? Will they thank Coleridge for this advocacy of Toryism?' Coleridge's exclusion from whatever idea conservatives have of their tradition is almost complete now; a number of recent books on the history of conservative thought leap from Burke directly to Disraeli, or, if Coleridge is mentioned at all, it is to be dismissed as unsystematic, confused, or mystical, in a tone which entitles us to suspect that he is not simply misunderstood—he is not read either. He can certainly be a difficult writer, and no doubt that is one reason why he was the first victim of the flight of English politics from ideology—another reason would be his contempt for the sort of pragmatic conservatism which finds its purest exponent, perhaps, in the present editor of *The Times*.

A comparable sense of futility overcomes an attempt to define Coleridge's influence on the Church in the nineteenth century. The Broad Church movement, which occupied the central position in the nineteenth-century Anglican Church, and which included at various times Thomas Arnold, Julius Hare, Maurice, Kingsley, Jowett, and, arguably, Carlyle, Tennyson and Browning, looked to Coleridge more than to anyone else as its instigator, and to *Aids to Reflection* and *Church and State* as its manuals. And yet so little have we to do now with questions of the Church that to explain that a particular work was once influential over the merely ecclesiastical, and even over the merely religious, aspects of the thought of however distinguished a body of men, is not to argue

* Colmer, *op. cit.*, p. 177.

very persuasively that the book is in immediate need of republication. If this is doubted, it should be considered how, when we discuss almost any book written before about 1900, we peel away the religious integuments of a writer's thought, in search of what appears to be its real or permanent content, the ideas which, abstracted from their religious context, and however distorted in the process, can still be of service in a secular culture. And however conscious we are of our responsibilities as historians or whatever to our material, it still seems to us that ideas of culture, for instance, that come to us from Thomas Arnold or F. D. Maurice, are of small value in the form in which they appeared to their originators, as ideas of religion. It is right, or at least inevitable, that we ignore so much of their meaning; but it does make the search for Coleridge's influence on the nineteenth-century Church an unrewarding one, however much stuff it turns up. If *Church and State* has any surviving influence, it is to be looked for instead in Coleridge's ideas of culture as they were taken up by John Stuart Mill and by Matthew Arnold. For Coleridge, of course, as much as for Thomas Arnold and Maurice, questions of culture and questions of religion were the same thing in the end, a position we can hardly adopt now, unless to argue that our culture, like our God, is dead. Mill and Matthew Arnold became the most important transmitters of the ideas of Coleridge precisely because they separated them from religious discussion and tried to refurbish them for a secular society; and in separating culture from religion, they tried to make (as has often been argued) a religion out of culture.

Mill had begun reading in Coleridge before his nervous breakdown, and before what he called 'the change in my opinions' in the late 1820s; but his serious interest in Coleridge began after that breakdown, during his long intellectual convalescence. What he found of value he described in his *Essay on Coleridge* which was published in 1840, and mainly concerned with *Church and State*; this essay is still by far the best introduction to Coleridge's political writings—'I might be thought to have erred in giving undue prominence to the favourable side', he wrote later. The problem for Mill was to reconcile the success of Coleridge, in many of the fields in which the Utilitarians were labouring, with the Utilitarian philosophy to which, by his father's efforts, he was almost naturally attuned. He tries to embrace both systems by a generous eclecticism, arguing with Leibniz that philosophic schools tend to be right in what they affirm and wrong in what they deny; but in doing this he is forced to argue (for example) that the Industrial Revolution was both good (following Bentham) and bad (following Coleridge), while evading the important question of whether its advantages outweighed its disadvantages, or for whom they did. He also argues that Utilitarianism can be successful in the purely business side of human affairs, while Coleridge is to be looked to for advice on questions of culture and of conscience; but this was more a separation than a reconciliation, with disturbing implications for the conduct of everyday life, and for the claim of Utilitarianism to provide a complete moral calculus—implications which Mill is pleased to acknowledge but not to examine.

This second attempt at synthesis was the one Mill adopted in practice, perhaps because it enabled him to immerse himself once more, and without asking awkward questions, in the business side of things; so that his views of the importance of Coleridge were no sooner crystallized in the 1840 essay than they dissolved. Mill is altogether less generous towards Coleridge in his *Essay on Representative Government* (1861); and any signs of an 'enlarged' or 'humanized' Utilitarianism will be looked for in vain in the *Principles of Political Economy*—where for Mill they would have been irrelevant, and where for Coleridge their absence would have been inexcusable. Such signs do appear, for example, in his 'Inaugural Address' as Rector of St Andrew's University (1867), in which he argues for the importance in education of the 'aesthetic branch', a 'department of things which deserves to be more regarded'. The aim of such education is to cultivate a 'tenderness of consciousness, to make us feel ourselves capable of nobler objects'; by the contemplation of natural scenery, for example, we are 'made to feel the puerility of petty objects which set men's interests at variance, contrasted with the nobler pleasures that all might share'. This is admirable, and the awkwardness of the language does not detract from the nobility of the aspiration; it does perhaps reveal, however, an embarrassment at setting so high a price on the pursuit of a cultural unity that has so little place in Mill's more important writings. It is usual to feel gratitude to Mill, for the genuine concessions he made to the importance of a moral and aesthetic education; but as Coleridge suggests in the remark on Locke, quoted earlier, the institutions of a culture are determined by the money which supports them, and Mill was no more able than anyone else, at his time or since, to argue the importance of culture in terms that were understood in the 'business world' that he understood. That our universities today are not exclusively polytechnics for the study of the mechanical and the social sciences is perhaps something to do with Mill's response to Wordsworth and Coleridge; but that they are becoming *almost* exclusively so is much to do with the philosophical movement of which he was in his time the most capable representative.

It was Coleridge who first directed our attention to 'culture' or 'cultivation', and he was the first writer in England to insist that the political health of a nation is inseparable from its cultural health. Among the already converted, the main guardian of these ideas from *Church and State* has been Matthew Arnold, and indeed, if they have survived at all, it is mainly via Arnold, who was immersed in the tradition of Coleridge's disciples. In *Culture and Anarchy* Arnold recommends culture as 'the great help out of our present difficulties'; and culture he defines as 'the general harmonious expansion of those gifts of thought and feeling which make the particular dignity, wealth, and happiness of human nature'. There is a clear memory here of Coleridge's definition of cultivation, and, like Coleridge, Arnold insists that this 'expansion' must be at once harmonious—the expansion of '*all* the powers which make the beauty and worth of human nature'—and general— 'the individual is required, under pain of being stunted and enfeebled in his own development if he disobeys, to carry others along with him in his march towards perfection'. Culture, as Arnold defines it further, is 'a pursuit of our total perfection by means of getting to know . . . the best which has been thought and said in the world'; and the agent by which a general culture is to be diffused must be the State, as the 'centre of light and authority'. We do not have such a State at the moment, Arnold says, because we live too much in our ordinary selves, in the pursuit of our individual and class interests; but within each social class there is a number of 'aliens' who are led 'not by their class spirit, but by a general *humane* spirit, by the love of human perfection'. These aliens live mainly in their 'best selves', and their influence must create a State as 'the organ of our collective best selves'.

There are other writers contributing to Arnold's ideas here— Burke, Carlyle, Wilhelm von Humboldt, as well as Coleridge. But the similarities with Coleridge extend beyond the definition of culture. Thus the notion of a 'remnant' of 'aliens' is clearly related to Coleridge's clerisy—an attempt, in the clear absence of a true clerisy in nineteenth-century England, to create such a class as an instrument for the diffusion of culture. But in noticing what survives from Coleridge, we should notice also what has been lost from the ideas of cultivation and of the clerisy in the forty years between the writing of *Church and State*, and the publication of *Culture and Anarchy*. One could sum it up, perhaps, by saying that however much Arnold insists that culture must be 'general', the tendency of his argument is strangely centripetal: the emphasis is on the State as the centre, and not (as in Coleridge) on the nation as a whole. I am not trying to make again here the objection often made against Arnold, that his notion of culture is a selfish one, the pursuit by the individual of his own perfection: Arnold is very wary of this pitfall, and emphatic that culture must be a *common* pursuit. But it seems to me that Arnold had no clear idea of what a general culture would be. Coleridge was explicit that the cultivation diffused by the clerisy was to be directed especially at teaching the members of a society their rights and obligations within that society, by making them aware of themselves as free moral agents who can exercise their freedom only as members of a society. Arnold has nothing like so sure a notion of the purpose of culture, and his strong words about the impossibility of pursuing one's own perfection in isolation seem to mean little more than that we should all pursue our individual perfection collectively; so that the pursuit of the thing is 'general', but not the thing itself. To put it another way: for Arnold, culture is something that leads to a right way of thinking in society, and a right way of acting, more valuable the more widely it is diffused. For Coleridge, cultivation is the very ground of a nation's existence: it is the development of our 'humanity'; we are truly human only as consenting members of a society; without that consent, or rather without the active pursuit of the cultivation which makes possible that consent, the nation ceases to exist.

In seeing how Coleridge's idea of cultivation was diluted by Arnold, we should remember that Coleridge was describing the National Church 'according to the idea'; Arnold's book has a more practical air, at least, and it is unfortunate that when he most dilutes what he derives from Coleridge, it is because he is trying, however half-heartedly, to translate his ideas into a programme of action. And unable to conceive of the State, or of culture, as expressions of our whole humanity in Coleridge's sense, he has to fall back on that idea of the State as the centre of the nation, as the organ, only, of our 'collective best selves'. Somehow our ordinary selves, for all the insistence on 'harmonious' expansion, 'total' perfection, cannot be saved by culture directly, but only as the dictates of culture are passed on to them by our best selves: they must submit to the authority of a State conceived as something like Rousseau's General Will, what we want whether we want it or not. It is the best self that culture seeks to develop, so that culture, like the State itself, is situated at the centre of the nation, the voice of an authority imposed on us by ourselves (or by the few cultured ones among us), and inevitably preserving the distinction between our best and our ordinary selves—Mill's 'aesthetic branch' and 'busi-

ness side' of things—which it would have been the task of
Coleridge's 'cultivation' to unify.

When Arnold was writing, the idea that culture was necessary
for the health of a nation was harder to argue than it had been
for Coleridge. In 1829 government was still in the hands of men
accustomed to paying lip-service, at least, to the importance of,
say, a 'grounding' in the Classics; by 1869 it was becoming the
fashion to ridicule 'culture', as a thing of no value for the
practical man. In the face of this hostility Arnold came to
defend an idea of culture much narrower than Coleridge's; and
if we ever think of the purpose of culture nowadays, it is in
Arnold's terms more than anyone else's—or in Coleridge's
terms only as they have been diluted by Arnold and by a number of later critics. This is true, even though we will hardly
find anyone in England today to defend even that reduced idea
of culture that Arnold offers; each new defence has involved
new concessions to whoever it is we think of as the enemies of
culture, so that now culture has no enemies at all; and criticism
of the preoccupation with the empirical sciences in education,
and with the 'art of the possible' in government, is at best a
pleasant and unobtrusive counterpoint to the hum of the
machine, and at worst only an expensive but tolerable absurdity.

A Bibliographical Note

Of Coleridge's works published during his lifetime, the most
immediately relevant to a study of *Church and State* are *The
Friend* (1809–10), which should be read in the edition of the
Bollingen Foundation; the two 'Lay Sermons', *The Statesman's
Manual* (1816) and '*Blessed are ye that sow beside all waters*'
(1817); and *Aids to Reflection* (1825). Apart from these,
Biographia Literaria (1817), *A Preliminary Treatise on Method*
(1818), *Specimens of Table Talk* (1835), the *Philosophical
Lectures*, ed. K. Coburn (Pilot Press, 1949), and *Coleridge on the
Seventeenth Century*, ed. R. F. Brinkley (Durham, N.C., 1955),
all contain ideas and suggestions developed in *Church and*

State. When Professor Coburn's edition of Coleridge's Note-books comes up to the 1820s, it will provide an indispensable commentary on the work. The best selection of Coleridge's political writings is R. J. White's *The Political Thought of Coleridge* (Cape, 1938).

For the first part of the book, Mill's excellent essay on Coleridge, available in various selections of Mill's work, is still the most useful introduction. Beyond that I would recommend particularly *Bentham, Coleridge, and the Science of History* (West Germany: Verlag Heinrich Pöppinghaus, 1958), by Robert O. Preyer, and David P. Calleo's *Coleridge and the Idea of the Modern State* (New Haven, 1966). An interesting and partly hostile review of *Church and State* appeared in the *Eclectic Review* (July 1831), and is reprinted in *Coleridge, The Critical Heritage*, ed. Jackson (Routledge, 1970). Raymond Williams's *Culture and Society* (Chatto, 1958) has some valuable pages on *Church and State*, as does John Colmer's *Coleridge, Critic of Society* (Oxford, 1959). There are some useful comments on Coleridge's ideas on education and the clerisy in the introduction to Wilkinson's and Willoughby's edition of Schiller's *Aesthetic Education* (Oxford, 1967). To his ideas on religion and theology, the best introduction is J. R. Barth's *Coleridge and Christian Doctrine* (Cambridge, Mass., 1969); C. R. Sander's *Coleridge and the Broad Church Movement* (Durham, N.C., 1942) and J. D. Boulger's *Coleridge as a Religious Thinker* (New Haven, 1961), are also useful. Thomas McFarland's *Coleridge and the Pantheist Tradition* (Oxford, 1969) has the best account so far of Coleridge's interest in F. H. Jacobi, whose spirit pervades the last two sections of *Church and State*.

ON THE CONSTITUTION

OF

THE CHURCH AND STATE,

ACCORDING TO

THE IDEA OF EACH;

WITH

AIDS TOWARDS A RIGHT JUDGMENT

ON THE LATE

CATHOLIC BILL.

BY S. T. COLERIDGE, ESQ., R.A., R.S.L.

ADVERTISEMENT.

THE occasion of this small volume will be sufficiently explained, by an extract from a letter to a friend:—"You express your wonder that I, who have so often avowed my dislike to the introduction even of the word, Religion, in any special sense, in Parliament, or from the mouth of Lawyer or Statesman, speaking as such; who have so earnestly contended, that Religion cannot take on itself the character of Law, without ipso facto ceasing to be Religion, and that Law could neither recognise the obligations of Religion for its principles, nor become the pretended Guardian and Protector of the Faith, without degenerating into inquisitorial tyranny—that I, who have avowed my belief, that if Sir Matthew Hale's[1] doctrine, that the Bible was a part of the Law of the Land, had been uttered by a Puritan Divine instead of a Puritan Judge, it would have been quoted at this day, as a specimen of puritanical nonsense and bigotry—you express your wonder, that I, with all these heresies on my head, should yet withstand the measure of Catholic *Emancipation*, and join in opposing Sir Francis Burdett's intended Bill, for the repeal of the disqualifying statutes![2] And you conclude by asking: but is this true?

"My answer is: Here are two questions. To the first, viz., is it true that I am unfriendly to (what is called) Catholic Emancipation? I reply: No! the contrary is the truth. There is no inconsistency, however, in approving the *thing*, and yet having my doubts respecting the manner; in desiring the same end, and yet scrupling the means proposed for its attainment. When you are called in to a consultation, you may perfectly agree with another physician, respecting the existence of the malady and the expedience of its removal, and yet differ respecting the medicines and the method of cure. To your second question (viz., am I unfriendly to the present measure?) I shall return an answer no less explicit. Why I cannot return as brief a one, you will learn from the following pages, transcribed, for the greater part, from a paper drawn up by me some years ago, at the request of a gentleman [3] (that I have been permitted to call him my friend, I place among the highest honours of my life), an old and intimate friend of the late Mr. Canning's; and which paper, had it been finished before he left England, it was his intention to have laid before the late Lord Liverpool.[4]

"From the period of the Union [5] to the present hour, I have neglected no opportunity of obtaining correct information from books and from men, respecting the facts that bear on the question, whether they regard the existing state of things, or the causes and occasions of it; nor, during this time, has there been a single speech of any note, on either side, delivered, or reported as delivered, in either House of Parliament, which I have not heedfully and thoughtfully perused, abstracting and noting down every argument that was not already on my list, which, I need not say, has for many years past few accessions to boast of. Lastly, my conclusion I have subjected, year after year, to a fresh revisal, conscious but of one influence likely to warp my judgment: and this is the pain, I might with truth add, the humiliation of differing from men, whom I loved and revered, and whose superior competence to judge aright in this momentous cause, I knew and delighted to know; and this aggravated by the reflection, that in receding from Burkes, Cannings, and Lansdownes,[6] I did not move a step nearer to the feelings and opinions of their antagonists. With this exception, it is scarcely possible, I think, to conceive an individual less under the influences of the ordinary disturbing forces of the judgment than your poor friend; or from situation, pursuits and habits of thinking, from age, state of health and temperament, less likely to be drawn out of his course by the undercurrents of Hope, or Fear, of expectation or wish. But least of all, by predilection for any particular sect or party: for wherever I look, in religion or in politics, I seem to see a world of power and talent wasted on the support of half truths, too often the most mischievous, because least suspected of errors. This may result from the spirit and habit of partizanship, the supposed inseparable accompaniment of a free state, which pervades all ranks, and is carried into all subjects. But whatever may be its origin, one consequence seems to be, that every man is in a bustle, and except under the sting of excited or alarmed self-interest, scarce any one in earnest."

I had written a third part[7] under the title of "What is to be done now?" consisting of illustrations from the History of the English and Scottish Churches, of the consequences of the ignorance or contravention of the principles, which I have attempted to establish in the first part: and of practical deductions from these principles, addressed chiefly to the English clergy. But I felt the embers glowing under the white ashes; and on reflection, I have considered it more expedient that the contents of this small volume should be altogether in strict conformity with the title; that they should be, and profess to be, no more and no other than *Ideas* of the Constitution in Church and State. And thus I may without inconsistency entreat the friendly reader to bear in mind the distinction I have ** enforced, between the exhibition of an idea, and the way of acting on the same; and that the scheme or diagram best suited to make the idea clearly understood, may be very different from the form in which it is or may be most adequately *realized*. And if the reasonings of this work should lead him to think, that a strenuous Opponent of the former attempts in Parliament may have given his support to the Bill lately passed without inconsistency, and without meriting the name of Apostate, it may be to the improvement of his charity and good-temper, and not detract a tittle from his good sense or political penetration.

S. T. C.

* p. 10.

1. Sir Matthew Hale (1609–76), Lord Chief Justice 1671–6. 'Hale's expression was "that Christianity is part of the laws of England; and therefore to reproach the Christian religion, is to speak in subversion of the law." *The King v. Taylor*. Ventr. 293, Keble, 607. But Sir Edward Coke had many years before said that "Christianity is part and parcel of the Common Law"' (H.N.C.).
2. Coleridge refers to the Emancipation Bill unsuccessfully introduced by Sir Francis Burdett (1770–1844) in May 1828. The Test Acts, disqualifying Catholics from holding civil and military office, and from sitting in Parliament, were passed in 1673 and 1678.
3. John Hookham Frere (1769–1846), politician, diplomat, and translator.
4. Lord Liverpool (1770–1828), Prime Minister 1812–27. Frere obtained from Liverpool the promise of a sinecure for Coleridge, but a stroke forced Liverpool to resign in 1827 and the project was forgotten. This was Coleridge's second attempt to interest Liverpool in his writings; he had sent the Prime Minister a copy of his *Lay Sermons*, but Liverpool complained that he 'did not well understand them'.
5. The Act of Union with Ireland was passed in 1800.
6. Burke had argued in favour of Catholic Relief in his *Letter to Sir Hercules Langrishe* (1792); George Canning (1770–1827), Prime Minister in 1827, had been a consistent if devious supporter of Emancipation; the third Marquis of Lansdowne (1780–1863) had introduced Burdett's unsuccessful 1828 bill into the Lords.
7. 'I had collected materials for a third part' (3rd edition).

ON THE CONSTITUTION

OF

THE CHURCH AND STATE,

ACCORDING TO

THE IDEA OF EACH.

There is a mystery in the soul of state,
Which hath an operation more divine
Than our mere chroniclers dare meddle with.

Shakespear.[1]

CHAPTER I.

Prefatory Remarks on the true import of the word, IDEA; *and what the author means by 'according to the Idea'.*

THE Bill [2] lately passed for the admission of Roman Catholics into the Legislature, comes so near the mark to which my convictions and wishes have through my whole life, since earliest manhood, unwaveringly pointed, and has so agreeably disappointed my fears, that my first impulse was to suppress the pages, which I had written while the particulars of the Bill were yet unknown, in compliance with the request of an absent friend, who had expressed an anxiety "to learn from myself the nature and grounds of my apprehension, that the measure would fail to effect the object immediately intended by its authors."

In answer to this, I reply, that the main ground of that apprehension is certainly much narrowed; but as certainly not altogether removed. I refer to the securities.[3] And, let it be understood, that in calling a certain provision hereafter specified, a *security*, I used the word *comparatively*, and mean no more, than that it has at least an equal claim to be so called, as any of those that have been hitherto proposed as such. Whether either one or the other deserve the name; whether the thing itself is possible; I leave undetermined. This premised,

I resume my subject, and repeat, that the main objection, from which my fears as to the practical results of the supposed Bill were derived, applies with nearly the same force to the actual Bill; though the fears themselves have, by the spirit and general character of the clauses, been considerably mitigated. The principle, the solemn recognition of which I deemed indispensable as a security, and should be willing to receive as the only security—superseding the necessity, though possibly not the expediency of any other, but itself by no other superseded— this principle is not formally recognized. It may perhaps be *implied* in one of the clauses (that which forbids the assumption of local titles by the Romish bishops); [4] but this implication, even if really contained in the clause, and actually intended by its framers, is not calculated to answer the ends, and utterly inadequate to supply the place, of the solemn and formal declaration which I had required, and which, with my motives and reasons for the same, it will be the object of the following pages to set forth.

But to enable you fully to understand, and fairly to appreciate, my arguments, I must previously state (what I at least judge to be) the true Idea of A CONSTITUTION; and, likewise, of a NATIONAL CHURCH. And in giving the essential character of the latter, I shall briefly specify its distinction from the Church of Christ, and its contra-distinction from a third form, which is neither national nor Christian, but irreconcileable with, and subversive of, both. By an *idea*, I mean, (in this instance) that conception of a thing, which is not abstracted from any particular state, form, or mode, in which the thing may happen to exist at this or at that time; nor yet generalized from any number or succession of such forms or modes; but which is given by the knowledge of *its ultimate aim*.

Only one observation I must be allowed to add, that this knowledge, or sense, may very well exist, aye, and powerfully influence a man's thoughts and actions, without his being distinctly conscious of the same, much more without his being competent to express it in definite words. This, indeed, is one of the points which distinguish *ideas* from *conceptions*, both

4

terms being used in their strict and proper significations. The latter, *i.e.* a conception, *consists* in a conscious act of the understanding, bringing any given object or impression into the same class with any number of other objects, or impressions, by means of some character or characters common to them all. *Concipimus*, id est, capimus hoc *cum* illo,[5]—we take hold of both at once, we *comprehend* a thing, when we have learnt to comprise it in a known *class*. On the other hand, it is the privilege of the few to possess an idea: of the generality of men, it might be more truly affirmed, that they are possessed by it.

What is here said, will, I hope, suffice as a popular explanation. For some of my readers, however, the following definition may not, perhaps, be useless or unacceptable. That which, contemplated *objectively* (*i.e.* as existing *externally* to the mind), we call a LAW; the same contemplated *subjectively* (*i.e.* as existing in a subject or mind), is an idea. Hence Plato often names ideas laws; and Lord Bacon, the British Plato, describes the Laws of the material universe as the Ideas in nature.[6] Quod in naturâ *naturatâ* LEX, in naturâ *naturante* IDEA dicitur.[7] By way of illustration take the following. Every reader of Rousseau, or of Hume's Essays,[8] will understand me when I refer to the Original Social Contract, assumed by Rousseau, and by other and wiser men before him, as the basis of all legitimate government. Now, if this be taken as the assertion of an historical fact, or as the application of a conception, generalized from ordinary compacts between man and man, or nation and nation, to an actual occurrence in the first ages of the world; namely, the formation of the first contract, in which men covenanted with each other to associate, or in which a multitude entered into a compact with a few, the one to be governed and the other to govern, under certain declared conditions; I shall run little hazard at this time of day, in declaring the pretended fact a pure fiction, and the conception of such a fact an idle fancy. It is at once false and foolish.* For what if an original contract had

* I am not indeed certain, that some operatical farce, under the name of a Social Contract or Compact, might not have been acted by the Illuminati [9] and Constitution-manufacturers, at the close of

actually been entered into, and formally recorded? Still I cannot see what addition of moral force would be gained by the fact. The same sense of moral obligation which binds us to keep it, must have pre-existed in the same force and in relation to the same duties, impelling our ancestors to make it. For what could it do more than bind the contracting parties to act for the general good, according to their best lights and opportunities? It is evident, that no specific scheme or constitution can derive any other claim to our reverence, than that which the presumption of its necessity or fitness for the general good shall give it; and which claim of course ceases, or rather is reversed, as soon as this general presumption of its utility has given place to as general a conviction of the contrary. It is true, indeed, that from duties anterior to the formation of the contract, because they arise out of the very constitution of our humanity, which supposes the social state—it is true, that in order to a rightful removal of the institution, or law, thus agreed on, it is required that the conviction of its inexpediency shall be as general, as the presumption of its fitness was at the time of its establishment. This, the first of the two great paramount interests of the social state demands, namely, that of permanence; but to attribute more than this to any fundamental articles, passed into law by any assemblage of individuals, is an injustice to their successors, and a high offence against the other great interest of the social state, namely,—its progressive improvement. The conception, therefore, of an original contract, is, we repeat, incapable of historic proof as a fact, and it is senseless as a theory.

But if instead of the *conception* or *theory* of an original social contract, you say the *idea* of an ever-originating social contract, this is so certain and so indispensable, that it constitutes the whole ground of the difference between subject and serf, between a commonwealth and a slave-plantation. And this,

---

the eighteenth century; a period which how far it deserved the name, so complacently affixed to it by the contemporaries of "this *enlightened* age", may be doubted. That it was an age of *Enlighteners*, no man will deny.

again, is evolved out of the yet higher idea of *person*, in contra-distinction from *thing*—all social law and justice being grounded on the principle, that a person can never, but by his own fault, become a thing, or, without grievous wrong, be treated as such: and the distinction consisting in this, that a thing may be used altogether and merely as the *means* to an end; but the person must always be included in the *end*: his interest must form a part of the object, a *means* to which, he, by consent, *i.e.* by his own act, makes himself. We plant a tree, and we fell it; we breed the sheep, and we shear or we kill it; in both cases wholly as means to *our* ends. For trees and animals are *things*. The wood-cutter and the hind are likewise employed as *means*, but on agreement, and that too an agreement of reciprocal advantage, which includes them as well as their employer in the *end*. For they are *persons*. And the government, under which the contrary takes place, is not worthy to be called a STATE, if, as in the kingdom of Dahomy,[10] it be unprogressive; or only by antici-pation, where, as in Russia, it is in advance to a better and more *man-worthy* order of things. Now, notwithstanding the late wonderful spread of learning through the community, and though the schoolmaster and the lecturer are abroad, the hind and the woodman may, very conceivably, pass from cradle to coffin, without having once contemplated this idea, so as to be conscious of the same. And there would be even an improba-bility in the supposition that they possessed the power of presenting this Idea to the minds of others, or even to their own thoughts, verbally as a distinct proposition. But no man, who has ever listened to laborers of this rank, in any alehouse, over the Saturday night's jug of beer, discussing the injustice of the present rate of wages, and the iniquity of their being paid in part out of the parish poor-rates,[11] will doubt for a moment that they are fully possessed by the idea.

In close, though not perhaps obvious connection, with this, is the idea of moral freedom, as the ground of our proper responsibility. Speak to a young Liberal, fresh from Edinburgh or Hackney or the Hospitals,[12] of Free-will, as implied in Free-agency, he will perhaps confess to you with a smile, that he is a

Necessitarian,—proceed to assure you that the liberty of the will is an impossible conception, *a contradiction in terms*,* and finish by recommending you to read Jonathan Edwards, or Dr. Crombie: or as it may happen, he may declare the will itself. a mere delusion, a non-entity, and ask you if you have read Mr. Lawrence's Lecture.[13] Converse on the same subject with a plain, single-minded, yet reflecting neighbour, and he may probably say (as St. Augustin had said long before him, in reply to the question, What is Time?)[14] I know it well enough when you do not ask me. But alike with both the supposed parties, the self-complacent student, just as certainly as with your less positive neighbour—attend to their actions, their feelings, and even to their words: and you will be in ill luck, if ten minutes pass without affording you full and satisfactory proof, that the *idea* of man's moral freedom possesses and modifies their whole practical being, in all they say, in all they feel, in all they do and are done to: even as the spirit of life, which is contained in no vessel, because it permeates all.

Just so is it with the † constitution. Ask any of our politicians what is meant by the constitution, and it is ten to one that he will give you a false explanation, *ex. gr.* that it is the body of our laws, or that it is the Bill of Rights; or perhaps, if he have read Tom Payne, he may tell you, that we have not yet got one; and yet not an hour may have elapsed, since you heard the same individual denouncing, and possibly with good reason, this or that code of laws, the excise and revenue laws, or those for including pheasants,[15] or those for excluding Catholics, as

* See AIDS TO REFLECTION, p. 226; where this is shewn to be one of the distinguishing characters of *ideas*, and marks at once the difference between an *idea* (a *truth-power* of the reason) and a conception of the understanding; viz. that the former, as expressed in words, is always, and necessarily, a *contradiction in terms*.

† I do not say, with the idea: for the constitution itself is an IDEA. This will sound like a paradox or a sneer to those with whom an Idea is but another word for *a fancy*, a something unreal; but not to those who in the ideas contemplate the most real of all realities, and of all operative powers the most *actual*.

8

altogether unconstitutional: and such and such acts of parliament as gross outrages on the constitution. Mr. Peel, who is rather remarkable for groundless and unlucky concessions,[16] owned that the present Bill breaks in on the constitution of 1688: and, A.D. 1689, a very imposing minority of the then House of Lords, with a decisive majority in the Lower House of Convocation, denounced the constitution of 1688, as breaking in on the English Constitution.[17]

But a Constitution is an idea arising out of the idea of a state; and because our whole history from Alfred onward demonstrates the continued influence of such an idea, or ultimate aim, on the minds of our fore-fathers, in their characters and functions as public men; alike in what they resisted and in what they claimed; in the institutions and forms of polity which they established, and with regard to those, against which they more or less successfully contended; and because the result has been a progressive, though not always a direct, or equable advance in the gradual realization of the idea; and that it is actually, though even because it is an *idea* it cannot be *adequately*, represented in a correspondent scheme of means really existing; we speak, and have a right to speak, of the idea itself, as actually existing, *i.e.*, as a *principle*, existing in the only way in which a principle can exist—in the minds and consciences of the persons, whose duties it prescribes, and whose rights it determines. In the same sense that the sciences of arithmetic and of geometry, that mind, that life itself, have reality; the constitution has real existence, and does not the less exist in reality, because it both *is*, and *exists as*, an IDEA.

There is yet another ground for the affirmation of its reality; that, as the fundamental idea, it is at the same time, the final criterion by which all particular frames of government must be tried: for here only can we find the great constructive principles of our representative system (I use the term in its widest sense, in which the crown itself is included as representing the unity of the people, the true and primary sense of the word majesty); those principles, I say, in the light of which it can alone be ascertained what are excrescences, symptoms of distemperature and marks of degeneration; and what are native growths, or changes naturally attendant on the progressive developement of the original germ, symptoms of immaturity perhaps, but not of disease; or at worst, modifications of the growth by the defective or faulty, but remediless, or only gradually remediable, qualities of the soil and surrounding elements.

There are two other characters, distinguishing the class of substantive truths, or truth-powers here spoken of, that will, I trust, indemnify the reader for the delay of the two or three short sentences required for their explanation. The first is, that in distinction from the *conception* of a thing, which being abstracted or generalized from one or more particular states, or modes, is necessarily posterior in order of thought to the thing thus conceived,—an idea, on the contrary, is in order of thought always and of necessity contemplated as antecedent. In the idea or principle, Life, for instance—the vital *functions* are the result of the organization; but this organization supposes and pre-supposes the vital *principle*. The bearings of the planets on the sun are determined by the ponderable matter of which they consist; but the *principle* of gravity, the *law* in the material creation, the *idea* of the Creator, is pre-supposed in order to the existence, yea, to the very conception of the existence, of matter itself.

This is the first. The other distinctive mark may be most conveniently given in the form of a caution. We should be made aware, namely, that the particular form, construction, or model, that may be best fitted to render the idea intelligible, and most effectually serve the purpose of an instructive *diagram*, is not necessarily the mode or form in which it actually arrives at realization. In the works both of man and of nature—in the one by the imperfection of the means and materials, in the other by the multitude and complexity of simultaneous purposes —the fact is most often otherwise. A naturalist, (in the infancy of physiology, we will suppose, and before the first attempts at comparative anatomy) whose knowledge had been confined exclusively to the human frame, or that of animals similarly organized; and who, by this experience had been led inductively to the idea of respiration, as the copula and mediator of the vascular and the nervous systems,—might, very probably, have regarded the lungs, with their appurtenants, as the only form in which this idea, or ultimate aim, was realizable. Ignorant of the functions of the spiracula in the insects, and of the gills of the fish, he would, perhaps, with great confidence degrade both to the class of non-respirants. But alike in the works of nature and the institutions of man, there is no more effectual preservative against pedantry, and the positiveness of sciolism, than to meditate on the law of compensation, and the principle of compromise; and to be fully impressed with the wide extent of the one, the necessity of the other, and the frequent occurrence of both.

Having (more than sufficiently, I fear,) exercised your patience with these preparatory remarks, for which the anxiety to be fully understood by you is my best excuse, though in a moment of less excitement they might not have been without some claim to your attention for their own sake, I return to the idea, which forms the present subject—the English Constitution, which an old writer calls, "Lex Sacra, Mater Legum, than which (says he), nothing can be proposed more certain in its grounds, more pregnant in its consequences, or that hath more harmonical reason within itself: and which is so connatural and essential to the genius and innate disposition of this nation, it being formed (silk-worm like) as that no other law can possibly regulate it—a law not to be derived from Alured, or Alfred, or Canute, or other elder or later promulgators of particular laws, but which might say of itself—When reason and the laws of God first came, then came I with them." [18]

As, according to an old saying, "an ill foreknown is half disarmed," I will here notice an inconvenience in our language, which, without a greater inconvenience, I could not avoid, in the use of the term *State*, in a double sense, a larger, in which it is equivalent to Realm and includes the Church, and a narrower, in which it is distinguised *quasi per antithesin* from the Church, as in the phrase, Church and State. But the context, I trust, will in every instance prevent ambiguity.[19]

1. *Troilus and Cressida*, III. iii. 210–13, adapted. The first of many misquotations in this work, most of them deliberate; 'mere chroniclers' is Coleridge's phrase, and they include (no doubt) David Hume and James Mill; the latter's *History of India* had appeared in 1818.

2. '10 G.IV. c. 7. "An Act for the relief of His Majesty's Roman Catholic subjects"' (H.N.C.).

3. These were mainly contained in Section 2 of the Act, and obliged Catholic peers and Catholics returned to the Commons to swear to defend the Protestant Succession, and not to disturb the Church Establishment or the Protestant Government, etc.

4. 'See ss. 24–5–6, prohibiting under a penalty the assumption of the titles of the bishoprics and other ecclesiastical dignities and offices; the exhibition of the *insignia* of Romish priesthood, and the performance of any part of Romish worship or religious service, elsewhere than in the usual chapels. These enactments have been openly violated with impunity from the passing of the Relief Act to this day'. (H.N.C.).

5. 'We *understand*, that is, we take this *together with* that.'

6. 'These are the true marks of the Creator on his creation, as they are impressed and defined in matter, by true and exquisite lines.' *Novum Organum*, I. 124; quoted in the original Latin by H.N.C.

7. 'That which in *created* nature is called a law, in *creative* nature is called an idea.' *Natura naturata* denotes the world of phenomena, of materialized form, apprehended, according to Coleridge, by the understanding; *natura naturans* denotes nature as the essence, the creative idea of the world, grasped only by the reason.

8. Coleridge must be thinking of Hume's Fifth Essay, in which however the Contract Theory appears in a very modified form: it is attractively simple, says Hume, but 'government commences more casually and more imperfectly'.

9. The 'Illuminati' ('Enlightened Ones') were members of a masonic, republican, deistical secret society founded by Adam Weishaupt in Bavaria in 1776. The term was adopted to describe other free-thinking groups of the eighteenth century, in this case perhaps the members of the French Constituent Assembly which produced the revolutionary constitution of 1791.

10. 'The Government of Dahomey is the most perfect despot-

ism . . . the policy of the country admits no intermediate degree of subordination between king and slave,' Archibald Dalzel, *History of Dahomey* (London, 1793), p. vii.

11. A reference to the Speenhamland system, whereby the wages of agricultural labourers were supplemented out of the poor-rates, according to a system of fixed allowances.

12. The most influential faculty at the University of Edinburgh at this time was that of Medicine, with a strong theoretical bias towards materialism and the 'mechanico-corpuscular' philosophy; the city was still a stronghold of utilitarian 'Scotch philosophers'. Hackney College was a 'Dissenting Academy'; no one could have been very fresh from Hackney in 1829, as it had been dissolved in 1796, after a member of the governing body had been imprisoned for 'attempted rebellion'; the college was materialist in philosophy and republican in politics. The 'Hospitals' are the teaching hospitals of London; the 'necessitarian' William Lawrence (see next note) was Surgeon at St Bartholomew's.

13. Jonathan Edwards (1703–58), American theologian. Edwards's necessitarianism was an aspect of his rigorous Calvinism, rather than a derivation from any materialist premisses; see especially his *A Careful & Strict Enquiry into the Modern Prevailing Notion of . . . Freedom of Will* (1754). Dr Alexander Crombie (1762–1840), philologist and philosopher; his *Defence of Philosophic Necessity* appeared in 1793. William Lawrence (1783–1867) was the author of two notorious series of lectures (*An Introduction to Comparative Anatomy and Physiology* and *On the Physiology, Zoology, and Natural History of Man*), described by contemporary theologians as attempts to undermine the foundations of religion.

14. *Confessions*, XI. 14.

15. A reference to the Game Laws.

16. Robert Peel (1788–1850) had resigned office in 1827 in opposition to the movement for Emancipation; in 1829, as a member of Wellington's government, he introduced the measure which became the Catholic Emancipation Act. The regular term for granting relief to Catholics was 'concession'; and Peel's was perhaps particularly 'groundless and unlucky', in that his change of policy was not based (as he explained himself) on any change of heart, but on an unwillingness to see the matter left 'un-

settled'. Coleridge detested Peel's pragmatism as thirty years earlier he had detested Pitt's.

17. In 1689 the Commons quickly agreed that James II had abdicated and that the throne was thereby vacant; it took two weeks for the Lords to be persuaded to agree to this formula, and an impressive minority voted in favour of adopting William of Orange as 'regent'. The Convocation of the Province of Canterbury assembled at the end of 1689, and the High Church Lower House refused William's request that it should debate a plan of 'Comprehension', to bring Dissenters nearer to the Anglican Church.

18. This quotation is adapted by Coleridge from remarks by Sir John Davies (1569–1626) on the Common Law, in the Preface Dedicatory (fourth page, pages unnumbered) to his *Report des Cases* (Dublin, 1615).

19. This paragraph was not included in the first edition.

CHAPTER II.

The idea of a State in the larger sense of the term, introductory to the constitution of the State in the narrower sense, as it exists in this Country.

A CONSTITUTION is the attribute of a state, *i.e.* of a body politic, having the principle of its unity within itself, whether by concentration of its forces, as a constitutional pure Monarchy, which, however, has hitherto continued to be *ens rationale*, unknown in history (*B. Spinozæ Tract. Pol. cap. VI. De Monarchiâ ex rationis præscripto*),[1]—or—with which we are alone concerned—by equipoise and interdependency: the *lex equilibrii*, the principle prescribing the means and conditions by and under which this balance is to be established and preserved, being the constitution of the state. It is the chief of many blessings derived from the insular character and circumstances of our country, that our social institutions have formed themselves out of our proper needs and interests; that long and fierce as the birth-struggle and the growing pains have been, the antagonist powers have been of our own system, and have been allowed to work out their final balance with less disturbance from external forces, than was possible in the Continental states.

> O ne'er enchain'd nor wholly vile,
> O Albion! O my Mother Isle!
> Thy valleys fair as Eden's bowers
> Glitter green with sunny showers!
> Thy grassy uplands' gentle swells
> Echo to the bleat of flocks;
> Those grassy hills, those glittering dells,
> Proudly ramparted with rocks:

15

> And OCEAN 'mid his uproar wild
> Speaks safety to his ISLAND-CHILD!
> Hence thro' many a fearless Age
> Has social Freedom lov'd the Land,
> Nor Alien Despot's jealous rage
> Or warp'd thy growth or stamp'd the servile Brand.
>
> ODE TO THE DEPARTING YEAR, *Dec.* 1796.[2]

Now, in every country of civilized men, acknowledging the rights of property, and by means of determined boundaries and common laws united into one people or nation, the two antagonist powers or opposite interests of the state, under which all other state interests are comprised, are those of PERMANENCE and of PROGRESSION.*

It will not be necessary to enumerate the several causes that combine to connect the permanence of a state with the land and the landed property. To found a family, and to convert his

* Permit me to draw your attention to the essential difference between *opposite* and *contrary*. Opposite powers are always of the same kind, and tend to union, either by equipoise or by a common product. Thus the + and — poles of the magnet, thus positive and negative electricity are opposites. Sweet and sour are opposites; sweet and bitter are contraries. The feminine character is *opposed* to the masculine; but the effeminate is its *contrary*. Even so in the present instance, the interest of permanence is opposed to that of progressiveness; but so far from being contrary interests, they, like the magnetic forces, suppose and require each other. Even the most mobile of creatures, the serpent, makes a *rest* of its own body, and drawing up its voluminous train from behind on this fulcrum, propels itself onward. On the other hand, it is a proverb in all languages, that (relatively to man at least) what would stand still must retrograde. You, my dear Sir, who have long known my notions respecting the power and value of words, and the duty as well as advantage of using them appropriately, will forgive this.

Many years ago, in conversing with a friend, I expressed my belief, that in no instance had the false use of a word become current without some practical ill consequence, of far greater moment than would *primo aspectu* have been thought possible. That friend, very wealth into land, are twin thoughts, births of the same moment, in the mind of the opulent merchant, when he thinks of reposing from his labours. From the class of the Novi Homines he redeems himself by becoming the staple ring of the chain, by which the present will become connected with the past; and the test and evidence of permanency afforded. To the same principle appertain primogeniture and hereditary titles, and the influence which these exert in accumulating large masses of property, and in counteracting the antagonist and dispersive forces, which the follies, the vices, and misfortunes of individuals can scarcely fail to supply. To this, likewise, tends the proverbial obduracy of prejudices characteristic of the humbler tillers of the soil, and their aversion even to benefits that are offered in the form of innovations. But why need I attempt to explain a fact which no thinking man will deny, and where the admission of the fact is all that my argument requires?

On the other hand, with as little chance of contradiction, I may assert, that the progression of a state, in the arts and comforts of life, in the diffusion of the information and knowledge, useful or necessary for all; in short, all advances in civilization, and the rights and privileges of citizens, are especially connected with, and derived from the four classes of the mercantile, the manufacturing, the distributive, and the professional. To early Rome, war and conquest were the substitutes for trade and commerce. War was their trade. As these wars became more frequent, on a larger scale, and with fewer interruptions, the liberties of the plebeians continued increasing: for even the sugar plantations of Jamaica would (in their present state, at least), present a softened picture of the hard and servile

---

lately referring to this remark, assured me, that not a month had passed since then, without some instance in proof of its truth having occurred in his own experience; and added, with a smile, that he had more than once amused himself with the thought of a verbarian Attorney-General, authorized to bring informations ex officio against the writer or editor of any work in extensive circulation, who, after due notice issued, should persevere in misusing a word.

relation, in which the plebeian formerly stood to his patrician patron.

Italy is supposed at present to maintain a larger number of inhabitants than in the days of Trajan or in the best and most prosperous of the Roman empire. With the single exception of the ecclesiastic state, the whole country is cultivated like a garden. You may find there every gift of God—only not freedom. It is a country, rich in the proudest records of liberty, illustrious with the names of heroes, statesmen, legislators, philosophers. It hath a history all alive with the virtues and crimes of hostile parties, when the glories and the struggles of ancient Greece were acted over again in the proud republics of Venice, Genoa, and Florence. The life of every eminent citizen was in constant hazard from the furious factions of their native city, and yet life had no charm out of its dear and honored walls. All the splendors of the hospitable palace, and the favor of princes, could not soothe the pining of Dante or Machiavel, exiles from their free, their beautiful Florence. But not a pulse of liberty survives. It was the profound policy of the Austrian and the Spanish courts, by every possible means to degrade the profession of trade; and even in Pisa and Florence themselves to introduce the feudal pride and prejudice of less happy, less enlightened countries. Agriculture, meanwhile, with its attendant population and plenty, was cultivated with increasing success; but from the Alps to the Straits of Messina, the Italians are slaves.

We have thus divided the subjects of the state into two orders, the agricultural or possessors of land; and the merchant, manufacturer, the distributive, and the professional bodies, under the common name of citizens. And we have now to add that by the nature of things common to every civilized country, at all events by the course of events in this country, the first is subdivided into two classes, which, in imitation of our old law books, we may intitle the Major and Minor Barons; both these, either by their interests or by the very effect of their situation, circumstances, and the nature of their employment, vitally connected with the permanency of the state, its institutions, rights, customs, manners, privileges—and as such, opposed to the inhabitants of ports, towns, and cities, who are in like manner and from like causes more especially connected with its progression. I scarcely need say, that in a very advanced stage of civilization, the two orders of society will more and more modify and leaven each other, yet never so completely but that the distinct character remains legible, and to use the words of the Roman Emperor, even in what is struck out the erasure is manifest.[3] At all times the lower of the two ranks, of which the first order consists, or the Franklins, will, in their political sympathies, draw more nearly to the antagonist order than the first rank. On these facts, which must at all times have existed, though in very different degrees of prominence or maturity, the principle of our constitution was established. The total interests of the country, the interests of the STATE, were entrusted to a great council or parliament, composed of two Houses. The first consisting exclusively of the Major Barons, who at once stood as the guardians and sentinels of their several estates and privileges, and the representatives of the common weal. The Minor Barons, or Franklins, too numerous, and yet individually too weak, to sit and maintain their rights in person, were to choose among the worthiest of their own body representatives, and these in such number as to form an important though minor proportion of a second House—the majority of which was formed by the representatives chosen by the cities, ports, and boroughs; which representatives ought on principle to have been elected not only by, but from among, the members of the manufacturing, mercantile, distributive, and professional classes.[4]

These four classes, by an arbitrary but convenient use of the phrase, I will designate by the name of the Personal Interest, as the exponent of all moveable and personal possessions, including skill and acquired knowledge, the moral and intellectual stock in trade of the professional man and the artist, no less than the raw materials, and the means of elaborating, transporting, and distributing them.

Thus in the theory of the constitution it was provided, that even though both divisions of the Landed Interest should combine in any legislative attempt to encroach on the rights and privileges of the Personal Interest, yet the representatives of the latter forming the clear and effectual majority of the lower House, the attempt must be abortive: the majority of votes in both Houses being indispensable, in order to the presentation of a bill for the Completory Act,—that is, to make it a law of the land. By force of the same mechanism must every attack be baffled that should be made by the representatives of the minor landholders, in concert with the burgesses, on the existing rights and privileges of the peerage, and of the hereditary aristocracy, of which the peerage is the summit and the natural protector. Lastly, should the nobles join to invade the rights and franchises of the Franklins and the Yeomanry, the sympathy of interest, by which the inhabitants of cities, towns, and sea-ports, are linked to the great body of the agricultural fellow-commoners, who supply their markets and form their principal customers, could not fail to secure a united and successful resistance. Nor would this affinity of interest find a slight support in the sympathy of feeling between the burgess senators and the country representatives, as members of the same House; and in the consciousness, which the former have, of the dignity conferred on them by the latter. For the notion of superior dignity will always be attached in the minds of men to that kind of property with which they have most associated the idea of permanence: and the land is the synonime of country.

That the burgesses were not bound to elect representatives from among their own order, individuals bonâ fide belonging to one or other of the four divisions above enumerated; that the elective franchise of the towns, ports, &c., first invested with borough-rights, was not made conditional, and to a certain extent at least dependent on their retaining the same comparative wealth and independence, and rendered subject to a periodical revisal and re-adjustment;[5] that in consequence of these and other causes, the very weights intended for the effectual counterpoise of the great land-holders, have, in the course of events, been shifted into the opposite scale; that they now constitute a large proportion of the political power and influence of the very class whose personal cupidity, and whose partial views of the landed interest at large they were meant to keep in check; these are no part of the constitution, no essential ingredients in the idea, but apparent defects and imperfections in its realization—which, however, we will neither regret nor set about amending, till we have seen whether an equivalent force had not arisen to supply the deficiency—a force great enough to have destroyed the equilibrium, had not such a transfer taken place previously to, or at the same time with, the operation of the new forces. Roads, canals, machinery, the press, the periodical and daily press, the might of public opinion, the consequent increasing desire of popularity among public men and functionaries of every description, and the increasing necessity of public character, as a means or condition of political influence—I need but mention these to stand acquitted of having started a vague and naked possibility in extenuation of an evident and palpable abuse.

But whether this conjecture be well or ill grounded, the *principle* of the constitution remains the same. That harmonious balance of the two great correspondent, at once supporting and counterpoising, interests of the state, its permanence, and its progression: that balance of the landed and the personal interests was to be secured by a legislature of two Houses; the first consisting wholly of barons or landholders, permanent and hereditary senators; the second of the knights or minor barons, elected by, and as the representatives of, the remaining landed community, together with the burgesses, the representatives of the commercial, manufacturing, distributive, and professional classes,—the latter (the elected burgesses) constituting the major number. The king, meanwhile, in whom the executive power is vested, it will suffice at present to consider as the beam of the constitutional scales. A more comprehensive view of the kingly office must be deferred, till the remaining problem (the idea of a national church) has been solved.

I must here intreat the reader to bear in mind what I have before endeavoured to impress on him, that I am not giving an historical account of the legislative body; nor can I be supposed to assert that such was the earliest mode or form in which the national council was constructed. My assertion is simply this, that its formation has advanced in this direction. The line of evolution, however sinuous, has still tended to this point, sometimes with, sometimes without, not seldom, perhaps, against, the intention of the individual actors, but always as if a power, greater, and better, than the men themselves, had intended it for them. Nor let it be forgotten that every new growth, every power and privilege, bought or extorted, has uniformly been claimed by an antecedent right; not acknowledged as a boon conferred, but both demanded and received as what had always belonged to them, though withheld by violence and the injury of the times. This too, in cases, where, if documents and historical records, or even consistent traditions, had been required in evidence, the monarch would have had the better of the argument. But, in truth, it was no more than a *practical* way of saying: this or that is contained in the *idea* of our government, and it is a consequence of the "Lex, Mater Legum," which, in the very first law of state ever promulgated in the land, was pre-supposed as the ground of that first law.

Before I conclude this part of my subject, I must press on your attention, that the preceding is offered only as the constitutional idea of the *State*. In order to correct views respecting the constitution, in the more enlarged sense of the term, viz. the constitution of the *Nation*, we must, in addition to a grounded knowledge of the *State*, have the right idea of the *National Church*. These are two poles of the same magnet; the magnet itself, which is constituted by them, is the CONSTITUTION of the nation.

1. i.e. *Tractatus Politicus*, VI (see esp. sect. v).
2. In Coleridge's *Poetical Works* (1828) the last three lines read: 'Has social Quiet lov'd thy shore;/Nor ever proud Invader's rage/Or sack'd thy towers, or stain'd thy fields with gore.'

3. See Suetonius, *Divus Claudius*, XVI. 1.
4. Coleridge refers to the control exercised by the Landed Interest over a large number of the borough seats in the unreformed House of Commons.
5. A reference to the 'rotten boroughs'.

CHAPTER III.

On the Church; i.e. the National Church.

THE reading of *histories*, my dear Sir, may dispose a man to satire; but the science of HISTORY,—History studied in the light of philosophy, as the great drama of an ever unfolding Providence,—has a very different effect. It infuses hope and reverential thoughts of man and his destination. To you, therefore, it will be no unwelcome result, though it should be made appear that something deeper and better than priestcraft and priest-ridden ignorance was at the bottom of the phrase, Church and State, and intitled it to be the form in which so many thousands of the men of England clothed the wish for their country's weal. But many things have conspired to draw off the attention from its true origin and import, and have led us to seek the reasons for thus connecting the two words, in facts and motives, that lie nearer the surface. I will mention one only, because, though less obvious than many other causes that have favoured the general misconception on this point, and though its action is indirect and negative, it is by no means the least operative. The immediate effect, indeed, may be confined to the men of education. But what influences these, will finally influence all. I am referring to the noticeable fact, arising out of the system of instruction pursued in all our classical schools and universities, that the annals of ancient Greece, and of republican and imperial Rome, though they are, in fact, but brilliant exceptions of history generally, do yet, partly from the depth and intensity of all early impressions, and in part, from the number and splendor of individual characters and particular events and exploits, so fill the imagination, as almost to be,—

during the period, when the groundwork of our minds is principally formed, and the direction given to our modes of thinking,—what we mean by HISTORY. Hence things, of which no instance or analogy is recollected in the customs, policy, and legisprudence of Greece and Rome, lay little hold on our attention. Among these, I know not one more worthy of notice, than the principle of the division of property, which, if not, as I however think, universal in the earliest ages, was, at all events, common to the Scandinavian, Celtic, and Gothic tribes, with the Semitic, or the tribes descended from Shem.

It is not the least among the obligations, which the antiquarian and the philosophic statist owe to a tribe of the last-mentioned race, the Hebrew I mean, that in the institutes of their great legislator, who first formed them into a *state* or nation, they have preserved for us a practical illustration of this principle in question, which was by no means peculiar to the Hebrew people, though in their case it received a peculiar sanction.

To confound the inspiring spirit with the informing word, and both with the dictation of sentences and formal propositions; and to confine the office and purpose of inspiration to the miraculous immission, or infusion, of novelties, rebus nusquam prius visis, vel auditis,[1]—these, alas! are the current errors of Protestants without learning, and of bigots in spite of it; but which I should have left unnoticed, but for the injurious influence which certain notions in close connexion with these errors have had on the present subject. The notion, I mean, that the Levitical institution [2] was not only enacted by an inspired Law-giver, not only a work of revealed *wisdom*, (which who denies?) but that it was a part of revealed *Religion*, having its *origin* in this particular revelation, as a something which could not have existed otherwise; yet, on the other hand, a part of the religion that had been *abolished* by Christianity. Had these reasoners contented themselves with asserting, that it did not *belong* to the Christian Religion, they would have said nothing more than the truth; and for this plain reason, that it forms no part of *religion* at all, in the Gospel sense of the word,

—that is, *Religion* as contra-distinguished from *Law*; spiritual, as contra-distinguished from temporal or political.

In answer to all these notions, it is enough to say, that not the principle itself, but the superior wisdom with which the principle was carried into effect, the greater perfection of the machinery, forms the true distinction, the *peculiar* worth, of the Hebrew constitution. The principle itself was common to Goth and Celt, or rather, I would say, to all the tribes that had not fallen off to either of the two *Aphelia*,[3] or extreme distances from the generic character of man, the wild or the barbarous state; but who remained either constituent parts or appendages of the *stirps generosa seu historica*,[4] as a philosophic friend has named that portion of the Semitic and Japetic[5] races, that had not degenerated below the *conditions* of progressive civilization:—it was, I say, common to all the primitive races, that in taking possession of a new country, and in the division of the land into hereditable estates among the individual warriors or heads of families, a reserve should be made for the nation itself.

The sum total of these heritable portions, appropriated each to an individual Lineage, I beg leave to name the PROPRIETY; and to call the *reserve* above-mentioned the NATIONALTY; and likewise to employ the term wealth, in that primary and wide sense which it retains in the term, Commonwealth. In the establishment, then, of the landed *proprieties*, a *nationalty* was at the same time constituted: as a *wealth* not consisting of lands, but yet derivative from the land, and rightfully inseparable from the same. These, the *Propriety* and the *Nationalty*, were the two constituent factors, the opposite, but correspondent and reciprocally supporting, counterweights, of the *commonwealth*; the existence of the one being the condition, and the perfecting, of the rightfulness of the other. Now as all polar forces, *i.e. opposite*, not *contrary*, powers, are necessarily *unius generis*, homogeneous, so, in the present instance, each is that which is called, relatively, by *predominance* of the one character or quality, not by the absolute exclusion of the other. The wealth appropriated was not so entirely a property as not to remain, to a certain extent, national; nor was the wealth reserved so exclusively national, as not to admit of individual tenure. It was only necessary that the mode and origin of the tenure should be different, and in *antithesis*, as it were. *Ex. gr.* If the one be hereditary, the other must be elective; if the one be lineal, the other must be circulative.

1. 'Things never seen or heard of before.'
2. See below, note 1, ch. IV.
3. 'Aphelia' are the points in the orbit of a planet or comet when it is at its furthest from the sun.
4. 'The noble stock, or that which partakes of history.'
5. The Japetic or Japhetic races inhabit Europe and North Asia, and are descended from Japheth, one of the sons of Noah.

CHAPTER IV.

Illustration of the preceding Chapter from History, and principally that of the Hebrew Commonwealth.

IN the unfolding and exposition of any idea, we naturally seek assistance and the means of illustration from the historical instance, in which it has been most nearly realized, or of which we possess the most exact and satisfactory records. Both of these recommendations are found in the formation of the Hebrew Commonwealth. But, in availing ourselves of examples from history, there is always danger, lest that, which was to assist us in attaining a clear insight into truth, should be the means of disturbing or falsifying it, so that we attribute to the object what was but the effect of flaws, or other accidents in the glass, through which we looked at it. To secure ourselves from this danger, we must constantly bear in mind, that in the actual realization of every great idea or principle, there will always exist disturbing forces, modifying the product, either from the imperfection of their agents, or from especial circumstances overruling them: or from the defect of the materials; or lastly, and which most particularly applies to the instances we have here in view, from the co-existence of some yet greater idea, some yet more important purpose, with which the former must be combined, but likewise subordinated. Nevertheless, these are no essentials of the idea, no exemplary parts in the particular construction adduced for its illustration. On the contrary, they are deviations from the idea, from which we must abstract, which we must put aside, before we can make a safe and fearless use of the example.

Such, for instance, was the settlement of the NATIONALTY in

one tribe,[1] which, to the exclusion of the eleven other divisions of the Hebrew confederacy, was to be invested with its rights, and to be capable of discharging its duties. This was, indeed, in some measure, corrected by the institution of the *Nabim*, or Prophets, who might be of any tribe, and who formed a numerous body, uniting the functions and three-fold character of the Roman Censors, the Tribunes of the people, and the sacred college of Augurs; protectors of the Nation and privileged state-moralists, whom, you will recollect, our Milton has already compared * to the orators of the Greek Democracies. Still the most satisfactory justification of this exclusive policy, is to be found, I think, in the fact, that the Jewish Theocracy itself was but a means to a further and greater end; and that the effects of the policy were subordinated to an interest, far more momentous than that of any single kingdom or commonwealth could be. The unfitness and insufficiency of the Jewish character for the reception and execution of the great legislator's scheme were not less important parts of the sublime purpose of Providence in the separation of the chosen people, than their characteristic virtues. Their frequent relapses, and the never-failing return of a certain number to the national faith and customs, were alike subservient to the ultimate object, the final cause, of the Mosaic dispensation. Without pain or reluctance,

* The lines which our sage and learned poet puts in the Saviour's mouth, both from their truth and from their appositeness to the present subject, well deserve to be quoted:—

> "Their orators thou then extoll'st, as those
> The top of eloquence:—Statists indeed
> And lovers of their country as may seem;
> But herein to our prophets far beneath,
> As men divinely taught and better teaching
> The solid rules of civil government,
> In their majestic, unaffected style,
> Than all the oratory of Greece and Rome.
> In them is plainest taught and easiest learnt
> What makes a nation happy, and keeps it so."
>
> Par. Reg. B. iv.[2]

therefore, I should state this provision, by which a particular lineage was made a necessary qualification for the trustees and functionaries of the reserved NATIONALTY, as the main cause of the comparatively little effect, which the Levitical establishment produced on the moral and intellectual character of the Jewish people, during the whole period of their existence as an independent state.

With this exception, however, the scheme of the Hebrew polity may be profitably made use of, as the diagram or illustrative model of a principle which actuated the primitive races generally under similar circumstances. With this and one other exception, likewise arising out of the peculiar purpose of Providence, as before stated, namely, the discouragement of trade and commerce in the Hebrew policy, a principle so inwoven in the whole fabric, that the revolution in this respect effected by Solomon [3] had no small share in the quickly succeeding dissolution of the confederacy, it may be profitably considered even under existing circumstances.

And first, let me observe, with the Celtic, Gothic, and Scandinavian, equally as with the Hebrew tribes, Property by absolute right existed only in a tolerated alien; and there was everywhere a prejudice against the occupation expressly directed to its acquirement, viz. the trafficking with the current representatives of wealth. Even in that species of possession, in which the right of the individual was the prominent relative character, the institution of the Jubilee [4] provided against its degeneracy into the merely *personal*; reclaimed it for the state,— that is, for the *line*, the *heritage*, as one of the permanent units, or integral parts, the aggregate of which constitutes the STATE, in that narrower and especial sense, in which it has been distinguished from the *nation*. And to these permanent units the calculating and governing *mind* of the state directs its attention, even as it is the depths, breadths, bays, and windings or reaches of a river, that are the subject of the hydrographer, not the water-drops, that at any one moment constitute the stream. And on this point the greatest stress should be laid; this should be deeply impressed, carefully borne in mind, that

the abiding interests, the *estates*, and ostensible tangible properties, not the *persons* as *persons*, are the proper subjects of the
state in this sense, or of the power of the parliament or supreme
council, as the representatives and plenipotentiaries of the state,
i.e. of the PROPRIETY, and in distinction from the commonwealth, in which I comprise both the Propriety and the
Nationalty.

And here permit me, for the last time, I trust, to encroach
on your patience, by remarking, that the records of the Hebrew
policy [5] are rendered far less instructive as lessons of political
wisdom, by the disposition to regard the Jehovah in that
universal and spiritual acceptation, in which we use the word as
Christians. But relatively to the Jewish polity, the Jehovah was
their covenanted king: and if we draw any inference from the
former, the Christian sense of the term, it should be this—that
God is the unity of every nation; that the convictions and the
will, which are one, the same, and simultaneously acting in a
multitude of individual agents, are not the birth of any individual; "that when the people speak loudly and unanimously,
it is from their being strongly impressed by the godhead or the
demon. Only exclude the (by no means extravagant) supposition of a demoniac possession, and *then* Vox Populi Vox Dei." [6]
So thought Sir Philip Sydney, who in the great revolution of
the Netherlands considered the universal and simultaneous
adoption of the same principles, as a proof of the divine
presence; and on that belief, and on that alone, grounded his
assurance of its successful result. And that I may apply this to
the present subject, it was in the character of the king, as the
majesty, or symbolic unity of the whole nation, both of the
state and of the persons; it was in the name of the KING, in
whom both the propriety and the nationalty ideally centered,
and from whom, as from a fountain, they are ideally supposed
to flow—it was in the name of the KING, that the proclamation
throughout the land, by sound of trumpet, was made to all
possessors: "The land is not your's, saith the Lord, the land is
mine. To you I lent it." [7] The voice of the trumpets is not,
indeed, heard in this country. But no less intelligibly is it

declared by the spirit and history of our laws, that the possession of a property, not connected with especial duties, a property not fiduciary or official, but arbitrary and unconditional, was in the light of our forefathers the brand of a Jew and an alien; not the distinction, not the right, or honour, of an English baron or gentleman.

1. The Levites. 'And, behold, I have given the children of Levi all the tenth in Israel for an inheritance, for . . . the service of the tabernacle of the congregation' (Numbers xviii. 21).
2. Lines 353–62.
3. See I Kings xi. 14–22.
4. The Jubilee occurred once every fifty years in Israel (see Leviticus xxv), when the land was left fallow, Hebrew slaves were emancipated, and lands that had been sold reverted to their former owners or their heirs.
5. 'Polity', 3rd edition, but the change (unless sanctioned by Coleridge) is unnecessary.
6. Quotation untraced, but see *F* (vol. IV. i, p. 182n) in which a part of the quotation also appears. The inverted commas disappear in the third edition, so the passage may conceivably be Coleridge's own. Sidney's opinion of the people of the Netherlands was generally less favourable: see *Prose Works*, pp. 149, 152.
7. The trumpet, and the (paraphrased) words of the Lord, from Leviticus xxv.

CHAPTER V.

Of the Church of England, or National Clergy, according to the Constitution; its characteristic ends, purposes and functions; and of the persons comprehended under the Clergy, or the Functionaries of the National Church.

AFTER these introductory preparations, I can have no difficulty in setting forth the right idea of a national church as in the language of Elizabeth the *third* great venerable estate of the realm. The first being the estate of the land-owners or possessors of fixed property, consisting of the two classes of the Barons and the Franklins; the second comprising the merchants, the manufacturers, free artizans, and the distributive class. To comprehend, therefore, this third estate, in whom the reserved nationalty was vested, we must first ascertain the end, or national purpose, for which it was reserved.

Now, as in the former state, the permanency of the nation was provided for; and in the second estate its progressiveness, and personal freedom; while in the king the cohesion by interdependence, and the unity of the country, were established; there remains for the third estate only that interest, which is the ground, the necessary antecedent condition, of both the former. Now these depend on a continuing and progressive civilization. But civilization is itself but a mixed good, if not far more a corrupting influence, the hectic of disease, not the bloom of health, and a nation so distinguished more fitly to be called a varnished than a polished people; where this civilization is not grounded in *cultivation*, in the harmonious developement of

33

those qualities and faculties that characterise our *humanity*. We must be men in order to be citizens.

The Nationalty, therefore, was reserved for the support and maintenance of a permanent class or order, with the following duties. A certain smaller number were to remain at the fountain heads of the humanities, in cultivating and enlarging the knowledge already possessed, and in watching over the interests of physical and moral science; being, likewise, the instructors of such as constituted, or were to constitute, the remaining more numerous classes of the order. This latter and far more numerous body were to be distributed throughout the country, so as not to leave even the smallest integral part or division without a resident guide, guardian, and instructor; the objects and final intention of the whole order being these—to preserve the stores, to guard the treasures, of past civilization, and thus to bind the present with the past; to perfect and add to the same, and thus to connect the present with the future; but especially to diffuse through the whole community, and to every native entitled to its laws and rights, that quantity and quality of knowledge which was indispensable both for the understanding of those rights, and for the performance of the duties correspondent. Finally, to secure for the nation, if not a superiority over the neighbouring states, yet an equality at least, in that character of general civilization, which equally with, or rather more than, fleets, armies, and revenue, forms the ground of its defensive and offensive power. The object of the two former estates of the realm, which conjointly form the STATE, was to reconcile the interests of permanence with that of progression—law with liberty. The object of the National Church, the third remaining estate of the realm, was to secure and improve that civilization, without which the nation could be neither permanent nor progressive.

That in all ages, individuals who have directed their meditations and their studies to the nobler characters of our nature, to the cultivation of those powers and instincts which constitute the man, at least separate him from the animal, and distinguish the nobler from the animal part of his own being, will be led by the *supernatural* in themselves to the contemplation of a power which is likewise super-*human*; that science, and especially moral science, will lead to religion, and remain blended with it— this, I say, will, in all ages, be the course of things. That in the earlier ages, and in the dawn of civility, there will be a twilight in which science and religion give light, but a light refracted through the dense and the dark, a superstition—this is what we learn from history, and what philosophy would have taught us to expect. But we affirm, that in the spiritual purpose of the word, and as understood in reference to a future state, and to the abiding essential interest of the individual as a person, and not as the citizen, neighbour, or subject, religion may be an indispensable ally, but is not the essential constitutive end of that national institute, which is unfortunately, at least improperly, styled a church—a name which, in its best sense is exclusively appropriate to the church of Christ. If this latter be ecclesia, the communion of such as are called out of the world, *i.e.* in reference to the especial ends and purposes of that communion; this other might more expressively have been entitled *enclesia*, or an order of men, chosen in and of the realm, and constituting an estate of that realm. And in fact, such was the original and proper sense of the more appropriately named CLERGY. It comprehended the learned of all names, and the CLERK was the synonyme of the man of learning. Nor can any fact more strikingly illustrate the conviction entertained by our ancestors, respecting the intimate connexion of this clergy with the peace and weal of the nation, than the privilege formerly recognized by our laws, in the well-known phrase, "benefit of clergy." [1]

Deeply do I feel, for clearly do I see, the importance of my Theme. And had I equal confidence in my ability to awaken the same interest in the minds of others, I should dismiss as affronting to my readers all apprehension of being charged with prolixity, while I am labouring to compress in two or three brief Chapters, the principal sides and aspects of a subject so large and multilateral as to require a volume for its full exposition. With what success will be seen in what follows, commencing with the Churchmen, or (a far apter and less objectionable designation,) the National CLERISY.

THE CLERISY of the nation,[2] or national church, in its primary acceptation and original intention comprehended the learned of all denominations;—the sages and professors of the law and jurisprudence; of medicine and physiology; of music; of military and civil architecture; of the physical sciences; with the mathematical as the common *organ* of the preceding; in short, all the so called liberal arts and sciences, the possession and application of which constitute the civilization of a country, as well as the Theological. The last was, indeed, placed at the head of all; and of good right did it claim the precedence. But why? Because under the name of Theology, or Divinity, were contained the interpretation of languages; the conservation and tradition of past events; the momentous epochs, and revolutions of the race and nation; the continuation of the records; logic, ethics, and the determination of ethical science, in application to the rights and duties of men in all their various relations, social and civil; and lastly, the ground-knowledge, the prima scientia as it was named,—PHILOSOPHY, or the doctrine and discipline * of *ideas*.

* That is, of knowledges immediate, yet real, and herein distinguished *in kind* from logical and mathematical truths, which express not realities, but only the necessary *forms* of conceiving and perceiving, and are therefore named the *formal* or *abstract* sciences. Ideas, on the other hand, or the truths of philosophy, properly so called, correspond to substantial beings, to objects whose actual subsistence is *implied* in their idea, though only *by* the idea revealable. To adopt the language of the great philosophic apostle, they are "*spiritual realities that can only spiritually be discerned*,"[3] and the inherent aptitude and moral *preconfiguration* to which constitutes what we mean by ideas, and by the presence of *ideal* truth, and of *ideal* power, in the human being. They, in fact, constitute his *humanity*. For try to conceive a *man* without the ideas of God, eternity, freedom, will, absolute truth, of the good, the true, the beautiful, the infinite. An *animal* endowed with a memory of appearances and of facts might remain. But the *man* will have vanished, and you have instead a creature, "more subtile than any beast

36

Theology formed only a part of the objects, the Theologians formed only a portion of the clerks or clergy of the national church. The theological order had precedency indeed, and deservedly; but not because its members were priests, whose office was to conciliate the invisible powers, and to superintend the interests that survive the grave; not as being exclusively, or even principally, sacerdotal or templar, which, when it did occur, is to be considered as an accident of the age, a mis-growth of ignorance and oppression, a falsification of the con-stitutive principle, not a constituent part of the same. No! The Theologians took the lead, because the SCIENCE of Theology was the root and the trunk of the knowledges that civilized man, because it gave unity and the circulating sap of life to all other sciences, by virtue of which alone they could be contemplated as forming, collectively, the living tree of knowledge. It had the precedency, because, under the name theology, were comprised all the main aids, instruments, and materials of NATIONAL EDUCATION, the *nisus formativus* [5] of the body politic, the shaping and informing spirit, which *educing, i.e.* eliciting, the latent *man* in all the natives of the soil, *trains them up* to citizens of the country, free subjects of the realm. And lastly, because to divinity belong those fundamental truths, which are the com-mon ground-work of our civil and our religious duties, not less indispensable to a right view of our temporal concerns, than to a rational faith respecting our immortal well-being. (Not without celestial observations, can even terrestrial charts be accurately constructed.) And of especial importance is it to the objects here contemplated, that only by the vital warmth diffused by these truths throughout the MANY, and by the guiding light from the philosophy, which is the basis of *divinity*, possessed by the FEW, can either the community or its rulers fully comprehend, or rightly appreciate, the permanent *distinction*, and the occasional

---

of the field, but likewise cursed above every beast of the field; upon the belly must it go and dust must it eat all the days of its life." [4] But I recall myself from a train of thoughts, little likely to find favour in this age of sense and selfishness.

contrast, between cultivation and civilization; or be made to understand this most valuable of the lessons taught by history, and exemplified alike in her oldest and her most recent records —that a nation can never be a too cultivated, but may easily become an over-civilized race.

1. 'Ecclesia' is derived from ἐκκαλεῖν, 'to call forth', 'to call out'. 'Enclesia' is, like 'clerisy' below, a coinage by Coleridge. 'Clergy', 'clerk', and 'clerisy' are all cognate with κλῆρος, 'that which is assigned by lot', or 'a heritable estate'. Coleridge would make the derivation depend on the clerk's having a *share* in the inheritance of the nationalty, but the O.E.D. is more impressed by the suggestion (see under 'cleric'), that the origin of the words is to be seen in Acts i. 17: τὸν κλῆρον τῆς διακονίας ταύτης, 'the lot of this ministry.'

2. In the first edition there was a parenthesis after 'nation': '(a far apter exponent of the thing meant, than the term which the usus et norma loquendi forces on me)'.

3. 1 Corinthians ii. 13f.

4. Genesis iii. 1 & 14.

5. 'Shaping power': the phrase is borrowed from the German physiologist Friedrich Blumenbach (1752–1840). 'The word *nisus* I have adopted chiefly to express an energy truly vital, and therefore to distinguish it as clearly as possible from powers merely mechanical'; Blumenbach, *Institutions of Physiology*, tr. Elliotson (London, 1817), p. 336n.

CHAPTER VI.

Secessions or offsetts from the National Clerisy. Usurpations and abuses previous to the Reformation. Henry VIII. What he might and should have done. The main End and Final Cause of the Nationalty; and the duties, which the State may demand of the National Clerisy. A question, and the answer to it.

As a natural consequence of the full developement and expansion of the mercantile and commercial order, which in the earlier epochs of the constitution, only existed, as it were, potentially and in the bud; the students and possessors of those sciences, and those sorts of learning, the use and necessity of which were indeed constant and perpetual to the *nation*, but only accidental and occasional to *individuals*, gradually detached themselves from the nationalty and the national clergy, and passed to the order, with the growth and thriving condition of which their emoluments were found to increase in equal proportion. Rather, perhaps, it should be said, that under the common name of professional, the learned in the departments of law, medicine, &c., formed an intermediate link between the established clergy and the burgesses.

This circumstance, however, can in no way affect the principle, nor alter the tenure, nor annul the rights of those who remained, and who, as members of the permanent learned class, were planted throughout the realm, each in his appointed place, as the immediate agents and instruments in the great and indispensable work of perpetuating, promoting, and increasing

39

the civilization of the nation, and who thus fulfilling the purposes for which the determinate portion of the total wealth from the land had been reserved, are entitled to remain its trustees, and usufructuary proprietors. But, remember, I do not assert that the proceeds from the nationalty cannot be rightfully vested, except in what we now mean by clergymen, and the established clergy. I have every where implied the contrary. But I do assert, that the nationalty cannot rightfully, and that without foul wrong to the nation it never has been, alienated from its original purposes. I assert that those who, being duly elected and appointed thereto, exercise the functions, and perform the duties, attached to the nationalty—that these collectively possess an unalienable, indefeasible title to the same —and this by a *Jure Divino*, to which the thunders from Mount Sinai might give additional authority, but not additional evidence.

COROLLARY.—During the dark times, when the incubus of superstition lay heavy across the breast of the living and the dying; and when all the familiar "tricksy spirits" in the service of an alien, self-expatriated and anti-national priesthood were at work in all forms, and in all directions, to aggrandize and enrich a "kingdom of this world;" large masses were alienated from the heritable proprieties of the realm, and confounded with the Nationalty under the common name of church property. Had every rood, every pepper-corn, every stone, brick, and beam, been re-transferred, and made heritable, at the Reformation, no right would have been invaded, no principle of justice violated. What the state, by law—that is, by the collective will of its functionaries at any one time assembled—can do or suffer to be done; that the state, by law, can undo or inhibit. And in *principle*, such bequests and donations were vitious *ab initio*, implying in the donor an absolute property in land, unknown to the constitution of the realm, and in defeasance of that immutable reason, which in the name of the nation and the national majesty, proclaims:—"The land is not yours; it was vested in your *lineage* in trust for the nation." And though, in change of times and circumstances, the interest of progression, with the means and motives for the same—Hope, Industry,

Enterprise—may render it the wisdom of the state to facilitate the transfer from line to line, still it must be within the same scale, and with preservation of the balance. The *most* honest of our English historians, and with no *superior* in industry and research, Mr. Sharon Turner, has labored successfully in detaching from the portrait of our first Protestant king the layers of soot and blood, with which pseudo-Catholic hate and pseudo-Protestant candour had coated it.[1] But the name of Henry VIII. would outshine that of Alfred, and with a splendor, which not even the ominous shadow of his declining life would have eclipsed—had he retained the will and possessed the power of effecting, what in part, he promised and proposed to do—if he had availed himself of the wealth, and landed masses that had been unconstitutionally alienated from the state, *i.e.* transferred from the scale of heritable lands and revenues, to purchase and win back whatever had been alienated from the opposite scale of the nationalty. *Wrongfully* alienated: for it was a possession, in which every free subject in the nation has a living interest, a permanent, and likewise a possible personal and reversionary interest! *Sacrilegiously* alienated: for it had been consecrated τῷ Θεῷ οἰκείῳ,[2] to the potential divinity in every man, which is the ground and condition of his *civil* existence, that without which a man can be neither free nor obliged, and by which alone, therefore, he is capable of being a free subject—a citizen.

If, having thus righted the balance on both sides, HENRY had then directed the nationalty to its true national purposes, (in order to which, however, a different division and sub-division of the kingdom must have superseded the present barbarism, which forms an obstacle to the improvement of the country, of much greater magnitude than men are generally aware of)—if the Nationalty had been distributed in proportionate channels, to the maintenance,—1, Of universities, and the great schools of liberal learning: 2, Of a pastor, presbyter, or *parson* * in every

---

* *i.e.* Persona κατ᾽ἐξοχήν;[3] persona *exemplaris*; the representative and exemplar of the *personal* character of the community or parish; of their duties and rights, of their hopes, privileges and

parish: 3, Of a school-master in every parish, who in due time, and under condition of a faithful performance of his arduous duties, should succeed to the pastorate; so that both should be labourers in different compartments of the same field, workmen engaged in different stages of the same process, with such difference of rank, as might be suggested in the names pastor and sub-pastor, or as now exists between curate and rector, deacon and elder. Both alike, I say, members and ministers of the national clerisy or church, working to the same end, and determined in the choice of their means and the direction of their labours, by one and the same object—namely, in producing and re-producing, in preserving, continuing and perfecting, the necessary sources and conditions of national civilization; this being itself an indispensable condition of national safety, power and welfare, the strongest security and the surest provision, both for the permanence and the progressive advance of whatever (laws, institutions, tenures, rights, privileges, freedoms, obligations, &c. &c.) constitute the public weal: these parochial clerks being the great majority of the national clergy, and the comparatively small remainder, being principally * *in* ordine *ad hos*, Cleri doctores ut Clerus Populi.[4]

---

requisite qualifications, as moral *persons*, and not merely living things. But this the pastoral clergy cannot be other than imperfectly —they cannot be that which it is the paramount end and object of their establishment and distribution throughout the country, that they should be—each in his sphere the germ and nucleus of the progressive civilization—unless they are *in the rule* married men and heads of families. This, however, is adduced only as an accessory to the great principle stated in a following page, as an instance of its beneficial consequences, not as the grounds of its validity.

* Considered, I mean, in their national relations, and in that which forms their *ordinary*, their most *conspicuous* purpose and utility; for Heaven forbid, I should deny or forget, that the sciences, and not only the sciences both abstract and experimental, but the Literæ Humaniores, the products of genial power, of whatever name, have an immediate and positive value, even in their bearings on the national interests.

I may be allowed, therefore, to express the final cause of the whole by the office and purpose of the greater part—and this is, to form and train up the people of the country to obedient, free, useful, organizable subjects, citizens, and patriots, living to the benefit of the state, and prepared to die for its defence. The proper *object* and end of the National Church is civilization with freedom; and the duty of its ministers, could they be contemplated merely and exclusively as officiaries of the *National* Church, would be fulfilled in the communication of that degree and kind of knowledge to all, the possession of which is necessary for all in order to their CIVILITY. By civility I mean all the qualities essential to a citizen, and devoid of which no people or class of the people can be calculated on by the rulers and leaders of the state for the conservation or promotion of its essential interests.

It follows therefore, that in regard of the grounds and principles of action and conduct, the State has a right to demand of the National Church, that its instructions should be fitted to diffuse throughout the people *legality*, that is, the obligations of a well-calculated self-interest, under the conditions of a common interest determined by common laws.[5] At least, whatever of higher origin and nobler and wider aim the ministers of the National Church, in some other capacity, and in the performance of other duties, might labour to implant and cultivate in the minds and hearts of their congregations and seminaries, should include the practical consequences of the *legality* above mentioned. The State requires that the basin should be kept full, and that the stream which supplies the hamlet and turns the mill, and waters the meadow-fields, should be fed and kept flowing. If this be done, the State is content, indifferent for the rest, whether the basin be filled by the spring in its first ascent, and rising but a hand's-breadth above the bed; or whether drawn from a more elevated source, shooting aloft in a stately column, that reflects the light of heaven from its shaft, and bears the "Iris, Cœli decus, promissumque Iovis lucidum," [6] on its spray, it fills the basin in its descent.

In what relation then do you place Christianity to the National

Church? Though unwilling to anticipate what belongs to a part of my subject yet to come, namely, the idea of the Catholic or Christian church, yet I am still more averse to leave this question, even for a moment, unanswered. And this is my answer.

In relation to the National Church, Christianity, or the Church of Christ, is a blessed * accident, a providential boon, a grace of God, a mighty and faithful friend, the envoy indeed and liege subject of another state, but which can neither administer the laws nor promote the ends of this other State, which is *not* of the world, without advantage, direct and indirect, to the true interests of the States, the aggregate of which is what we † mean by the WORLD—*i.e.* the civilized world. As the olive tree is said in its growth to fertilize the surrounding soil; to invigorate the roots of the vines in its immediate neighbourhood, and to improve the strength and flavour of the wines— such is the relation of the Christian and the National Church. But as the olive is not the same plant with the vine, or with the elm or poplar (*i.e.* the State) with which the vine is wedded; and as the vine with its prop may exist, though in less perfection, without the olive, or prior to its implantation—even so is Christianity, and à fortiori any particular scheme of Theology derived and supposed (by its partizans) to be *deduced* from Christianity, no essential part of the *Being* of the *National* Church, however conducive or even indispensable it may be to its *well* being. And even so a National Church might exist,

* Let not the religious reader be offended with this phrase. The writer means only that Christianity is an aid and instrument, which no State or Realm could have produced out of its own elements— which no State had a right to expect. It was, most awfully, a GOD-SEND!

† What we ought to mean, at least: for I blush to think, current as the term is among the religious public in consequence of its frequent occurrence in the New Testament, how many discourses I have heard, in which the preacher has made it only too evident that he understood by the term the earth which turns round with us, the planet TELLUS of the astronomers!

44

and has existed, without, because before the institution of the *Christian* Church—as the Levitical Church in the Hebrew Constitution, the Druidical in the Celtic, would suffice to prove.

But here I earnestly intreat, that two things may be remembered—first, that it is my object to present the *Idea* of a National Church, as the only safe criterion, by which the judgment can decide on the existing state of things; for when we are in full and clear possession of the ultimate aim of an Institution, it is comparatively easy to ascertain, in what respects this aim has been attained in other ways, arising out of the growth of the Nation, and the gradual and successive expansion of its germs; in what respects the aim has been frustrated by errors and diseases in the body politic; and in what respects the existing institution still answers the original purpose, and continues to be a mean to necessary or most important ends, for which no adequate substitute can be found. First, I say, let it be borne in mind, that my object has been to present the *idea* of a National Church, not the history of *the* Church established in this nation. Secondly, that two distinct functions do not necessarily imply or require two different functionaries. Nay, the perfection of each may require the union of both in the same person. And in the instance now in question, great and grievous errors have arisen from confounding the functions; and fearfully great and grievous will be the evils from the success of an attempt to separate them—an attempt long and passionately pursued, in many forms, and through many various channels, by a numerous party, who has already the ascendancy in the *State*; and which, unless far other minds and far other principles than the opponents of this party have hitherto allied with their cause, are called into action, *will* obtain the ascendancy in the *Nation*.[7]

I have already said, that the subjects, which lie right and left of my road, or even jut into it, are so many and so important, that I offer these Chapters but as a catalogue *raisonné* of texts and theses, that will have answered their purpose if they excite a certain class of readers to desire or to supply the commentary. But there will not be wanting among my readers men who are no strangers to the ways, in which my thoughts travel: and the jointless sentences that make up the following Chapter or Inventory of regrets and apprehensions, will suffice to possess them of the chief points that press on my mind.

The [8] commanding knowledge, the *power* of truth, given or obtained by contemplating the subject in the fontal mirror of the Idea, is in Scripture ordinarily expressed by Vision: and no dissimilar gift, if not rather in its essential characters the same, does a great living Poet speak of, as

"The VISION and the Faculty divine." [9]

And of the many political *ground-truths* contained in the Old Testament, I cannot recall one more worthy to be selected as the *Moral* and L'ENVOY of a Universal History, than the text in Proverbs, WHERE NO VISION IS, THE PEOPLE PERISHETH.[10]

It is now thirty years since the diversity of REASON and the UNDERSTANDING, of an Idea and a Conception, and the practical importance of distinguishing the one from the other, were first made evident to me. And scarcely a month has passed during this long interval in which either books, or conversation, or the experience of life, have not supplied or suggested some fresh proof and instance of the mischiefs and mistakes, derived from that ignorance of this Truth, which I have elsewhere called the Queen-bee in the Hive of Error.

Well and truly has the understanding been defined; *Facultas mediata et Mediorum :*[11]—the Faculty of means to medial Ends, that is to *Purposes*, or such ends as are themselves but means to some ulterior end.

My eye at this moment rests on a volume newly read by me, containing a well-written history of the Inventions, Discoveries, Public Improvements, Docks, Rail-ways, Canals, &c. for about the same period, in England and Scotland. I closed it under the strongest impressions of awe, and admiration akin to wonder. We live, I exclaimed, under the dynasty of the understanding: and this is its golden age.

It is the faculty of means to medial ends. With these the age, this favoured land, teems: they spring up, the armed host, ("seges clypeata") from the serpent's teeth sown by Cadmus: "mortalia semina, dentes." [12] In every direction they advance, conquering and to conquer. Sea, and Land, Rock, Mountain, Lake and Moor, yea Nature and all her Elements, sink before them, or yield themselves captive! But the *ultimate* ends? Where shall I seek for information concerning these? By what name shall I seek for the historiographer of REASON? Where shall I find the annals of *her* recent campaigns? the records of her conquests? In the facts disclosed by the Mendicant Society? [13] In the reports on the increase of crimes, commitments? In the proceedings of the Police? Or in the accumulating volumes on the horrors and perils of population?

> "O voice, once heard
> Delightfully, *Increase and multiply!*
> Now death to hear! For what can we increase
> Or multiply, *but penury, woe and crime?*"
>
> PAR. LOST.[14]

Alas! for a certain class, the following Chapter will, I fear, but too vividly shew "the burden of the valley of vision, even the burden upon the crowned isle, whose merchants are princes, whose traffickers the honourable of the earth; who stretcheth out her hand over the sea, and she is the mart of nations!" (Isaiah, xxiii.)

1. Sharon Turner (1768–1847), whose *History of the Reign of Henry VIII* was published in 1826.
2. 'To God within each of us individually.'
3. '*Par excellence*'.
4. 'In respect to those (i.e., to the majority of the national clergy), teachers of the cleric as the cleric is the people's teacher.' The phrase *in ordine ad* translates the English 'in order to' in the obsolete meaning given by the O.E.D. (see under 'order'), and used often by Coleridge in this work (e.g. in the next paragraph).
5. 'under the conditions . . . common laws', 2nd and 3rd editions; 'enlivened by the affections and the warrantable prejudices of nationality', 1st edition.

6. 'Iris, glory of Heaven, and bright promise of Jove'; cf. *Aeneid* IX. 18.
7. A reference to the increasing pressure, from Dissenters, Catholics, and Utilitarians, for non-denominational elementary education.
8. This paragraph and the four following not in first edition.
9. Wordsworth, *Excursion*, I. 79.
10. Proverbs xxix. 18.
11. If this is the definition of another writer, I have been unable to trace it; Coleridge speaks himself of the understanding as 'the faculty of means to proximate or medial ends' in *AR*, p. 250n.
12. 'A shield-bearing crop'; 'teeth which are seeds, and produce men'; see Ovid, *Metamorphoses*, III. 105–10.
13. The 'Mendicant Society' (more properly the Society for the Suppression of Mendicity), established in 1818, published annual reports on its dealings with the deserving and the undeserving poor.
14. Book X. 729–32, altered.

CHAPTER VII.

Regrets and Apprehensions.

THE National Church was deemed in the *dark age* of Queen Elizabeth, in the unenlightened times of Burleigh, Hooker, Spenser, Shakspeare, and Lord Bacon, A GREAT VENERABLE ESTATE OF THE REALM; but now by " *all* the intellect of the kingdom," it has been determined to be one of the many theological sects, churches or communities, established in the realm; but distinguished from the rest by having its priesthood *endowed*, durante bene placito,[1] by favour of the legislature—that is, of the majority, for the time being, of the two Houses of Parliament. The Church being thus reduced to *a* religion, Religion *in genere* is consequently separated from the church, and made a subject of parliamentary determination, independent of this church. The poor withdrawn from the discipline of the church. The education of the people detached from the ministry of the church. Religion, a *noun of multitude*, or nomen collectivum, expressing the aggregate of all the different groups of notions and ceremonies connected with the invisible and supernatural. On the plausible (and in *this* sense of the word, unanswerable) pretext of the multitude and variety of *Religions*, and for the suppression of bigotry and negative persecution, National Education to be finally sundered from all religion, but speedily and decisively emancipated from the superintendence of the National Clergy.[2] Education reformed. Defined as synonimous with Instruction. *Axiom of Education so defined.* Knowledge being power, those attainments, which give a man the power of doing what he wishes in order to obtain what he desires, are alone to be considered as knowledge, or to be admitted into the

49

scheme of National Education. Subjects to be taught in the National Schools.[3] Reading, writing, arithmetic, the mechanic arts, elements and results of physical science, but to be taught, as much as possible, empirically. For all knowledge being derived from the Senses, the closer men are kept to the fountain head, the *knowinger* they must become.—POPULAR ETHICS, *i.e.* a Digest of the Criminal Laws, and the evidence requisite for conviction under the same: Lectures on Diet, on Digestion, on Infection, and the nature and effects of a specific virus incidental to and communicable by living bodies in the intercourse of society. N.B. In order to balance the Interests of Individuals and the Interests of the State, the Dietetic and Peptic Text Books, to be under the censorship of the Board of Excise.

Shall I proceed with my chapter of hints? Game Laws, Corn Laws, Cotton Factories, Spitalfields,[4] the tillers of the land paid by poor-rates, and the remainder of the population mechanized into engines for the manufactory of new rich men—yea, the machinery of the wealth of the nation made up of the wretchedness, disease and depravity of those who should constitute the strength of the nation! Disease, I say, and vice, while the wheels are in full motion; but at the first stop the magic wealth-machine is converted into an intolerable weight of pauperism! But this partakes of History. The head and neck of the huge Serpent are out of the den: the voluminous train is to come. What next? May I not whisper as a fear, what Senators have promised to demand as a right? Yes! the next in my filial bodings is Spoliation.—Spoliation of the NATIONALTY, half thereof to be distributed among the land-owners, and the other half among the stock-brokers, and stock-owners, who are to receive it in lieu of the interest formerly due to them.

But enough! I will ask only one question. Has the national welfare, have the *weal* and happiness of the people, advanced with the increase of the circumstantial prosperity? Is the increasing number of wealthy individuals that which ought to be understood by the wealth of the nation? In answer to this, permit me to annex the following chapter of contents of the moral history of the last 130 years.

A. Declarative act, respecting certain parts of the constitution, with provisions against further violation of the same, erroneously entitled, "THE REVOLUTION of 1688." [5]

B. The Mechanico-corpuscular Theory [6] raised to the Title of the Mechanic Philosophy, and espoused as a revolution in philosophy, by the actors and partizans of the (so called) Revolution in the state.

C. Result illustrated, in the remarkable contrast between the acceptation of the word, Idea, *before* the Restoration, and the *present* use of the same word. *Before* 1660, the magnificent SON OF COSMO was wont to discourse with FICINO, POLITIAN and the princely MIRANDULA on the IDEAS of Will, God, Freedom.[7] SIR PHILIP SIDNEY, the star of serenest brilliance in the glorious constellation of Elizabeth's court, communed with SPENSER, on the IDEA of the beautiful; and the younger ALGERNON— Soldier, Patriot, and Statesman—with HARRINGTON, MILTON, and NEVIL on the IDEA of the STATE: [8] and in what sense it may be more truly affirmed, that the people (*i.e.* the component particles of the body politic, at any moment existing as such) are in order to the state, than that the state exists for the sake of the people.

Present use of the word.

DR. HOLOFERNES,[9] in a lecture on metaphysics, delivered at one of the Mechanics' Institutions,[10] explodes all *ideas* but those of sensation; and his friend, DEPUTY COSTARD, has no *idea* of a better flavored haunch of venison, than he dined off at the London Tavern last week. He admits, (for the deputy has travelled) that the French have an excellent *idea* of cooking in general; but holds that their most accomplished *Maîtres de Cuisine* have no more *idea* of dressing a turtle, than the Parisian Gourmands themselves have any *real* idea of the true *taste* and *colour* of the fat.

D. Consequences exemplified. State of nature, or the Ouran Outang [11] theology of the origin of the human race, substituted for the Book of Genesis, ch. I.——X. Rights of nature for the duties and privileges of citizens. Idealess facts, misnamed proofs from history, grounds of experience, &c., substituted for principles and the insight derived from them. State-policy, a Cyclops with one eye, and that in the back of the head! Our measures of policy, either a series of anachronisms, or a truckling to events substituted for the science, that should command them; for all true insight is foresight. (Documents. The measures of the British Cabinet from the Boston Port-Bill, March, 1774; [12] but particularly from 1789, to the Union of Ireland, and the Peace of Amiens.[13]) Mean time, the true historical feeling, the immortal life of an historical Nation, generation linked to generation by faith, freedom, heraldry, and ancestral fame, languishing, and giving place to the superstitions of wealth, and newspaper reputation.

E. Talents without genius: a swarm of clever, well-informed men: an anarchy of minds, a despotism of maxims. Despotism of finance in government and legislation—of vanity and sciolism in the intercourse of life—of presumption, temerity, and hardness of heart, in political economy.

F. The Guess-work of general consequences substituted for moral and political philosophy, adopted as a text book in one of the Universities,[14] and cited, as authority, in the legislature: Plebs pro Senatu Populoque; [15] the wealth of the nation (*i.e.* of the wealthy individuals thereof, and the magnitude of the Revenue) for the well-being of the people.

G. Gin consumed by paupers to the value of about eighteen millions yearly. Government by journeymen clubs; [16] by saint and sinner societies, [17] committees, institutions; by reviews, magazines, and above all by newspapers. Lastly, crimes quadrupled for the whole country, and in some counties decupled.

Concluding address to the parliamentary leaders of the Liberalists and Utilitarians. I respect the talents of many, and the motives and character of some among you too sincerely to court the scorn, which I anticipate. But neither shall the fear of it prevent me from declaring aloud, and as a truth which I hold it the disgrace and calamity of a professed statesman not to know and acknowledge, that a permanent, nationalized, learned order, a national clerisy or church, is an essential element of a rightly constituted nation, without which it wants the best security alike for its permanence and its progression; and for which neither tract societies nor conventicles, nor Lancasterian schools,[18] nor mechanics' institutions, nor lecture-bazaars under the absurd name of universities,[19] nor all these collectively, can be a substitute. For they are all marked with the same asterisk of spuriousness,[20] shew the same distemper-spot on the front, that they are empirical specifics for morbid *symptoms* that help to feed and continue the disease.

But you wish for *general* illumination: you would spur-arm the toes of society: you would enlighten the higher ranks per ascensum ab imis.[21] You begin, therefore, with the attempt to *popularize* science: but you will only effect its *plebification*. It is folly to think of making all, or the many, philosophers, or even men of science and systematic knowledge. But it is duty and wisdom to aim at making as many as possible soberly and steadily religious;—inasmuch as the morality which the state requires in its citizens for its own well-being and ideal immortality, and without reference to their spiritual interests as individuals, can only exist for the people in the form of religion. But the existence of a true philosophy, or the power and habit of contemplating particulars in the unity and fontal mirror of the idea—this in the rulers and teachers of a nation is indispensable to a sound state of religion in all classes. In fine, Religion, true or false, is and ever has been the centre of gravity in a realm, to which all other things must and will accommodate themselves.

1. 'During our good pleasure': the condition under which certain official positions are given by the Crown.
2. Coleridge may refer to the opposition to Brougham's Parish Schools Bill of 1820, which proposed that schools should be erected by manufacturers, supported by the rates, and super-

vised by the Minister and Vestry of each parish. It was hotly opposed by Catholics and Dissenters, supported only luke-warmly by the Church, and withdrawn.

3. The National Schools, run by the 'National Society for Promoting the Education of the Poor in the Principles of the Established Church', did include a good deal of the religion of the prayer-book and catechism in their curriculum. Coleridge may be thinking more of their rivals, the British Schools of Joseph Lancaster (see below, note 18), in which religious instruction was 'undenominational', and confined mainly to Bible-reading.

4. After 1824, when the 'Spitalfields Acts' regulating the wages of silk-weavers were repealed, that part of London became notorious for strikes and other more direct forms of industrial action, such as window-breaking, cutting silk on the loom, etc.

5. The Bill of Rights, which was passed in 1689 by the Convention Parliament, a legislative body of doubtful authority in that it was summoned by William of Orange before he became king. The Convention resolved that James II had abdicated, and that the crown should be offered to William and Mary. It was followed in 1690 by a new parliament which confirmed the statutes made by the Convention. It is this series of events that (to the constitutional historian) makes up the 'Revolution of 1688'.

6. i.e., that of Locke and Newton especially.

7. Lorenzo de Medici (1449–92), Marsilio Ficino (1433–1499), Angelo Poliziano (1454–1494) and Pico, Count of Mirandola (1463–94), all members of the Platonic Academy of Florence.

8. This communion is probably imagined as taking place at the Rota, a platonic, aristocratic, republican political discussion club founded by Sir James Harrington (1611–77), the author of *The Commonwealth of Oceana* (1656), and attended by Henry Nevil (1620–94), whose *Plato Redivivus* appeared in 1681. Algernon Sidney (1622–83), republican political theorist (and the great-nephew of Sir Philip), was executed on account of the ideas advanced in his then unpublished 'Discourses concerning Government'.

9. For Holofernes and Costard, see *Love's Labour's Lost*.

10. These were institutions set up to instruct artisans in 'such

branches of physical science as are of practical advantage in their several trades'; there were over 100 by 1826.

11. The theory that the orang-utan was the natural and original man was put forward most notably by James Burnett, Lord Monboddo (1714–99) in his *Origin and Progress of Language* (1773–92).

12. An act to close the port at Boston until the town had made good the losses suffered by the East India Company at the Boston Tea-Party.

13. The Act of Union (1800) was passed as an *ad hoc* attempt to pacify Ireland after the rebellion of the 1790s; by the Treaty of Amiens (1802) the British Government agreed to restore virtually all its conquests to France and Spain, in return for several insignificant concessions.

14. William Paley's *Principles of Moral and Political Philosophy*, a work of christianized Utilitarianism, was published in 1785 and immediately adopted as a text-book at Cambridge. 'General consequences' is a phrase from Paley.

15. 'The populace for the senate and the people': *plebs* denotes the people understood as lacking any unifying principle; *populus*, the people as having an organized political identity.

16. Embryonic trade unions, or Trade Friendly Societies.

17. Evangelical societies.

18. 'Conventicles': meetings (or meeting-places) of non-conformists; the term became opprobrious in some quarters after the late seventeenth century, when two acts were passed to suppress 'seditious conventicles'. 'Lancasterian Schools' were founded by Joseph Lancaster (1778–1838), the Quaker educationalist and advocate of the 'monitorial system.'

19. This is identified by the reviewer of *Church and State* in the *Eclectic Review* (July 1831) as a reference to King's College, London, founded in 1829; but Coleridge may also refer to University College, already in 1829 (erroneously) styled the 'University of London'.

20. An asterisk is used by classical scholars to indicate that a work attributed by tradition to a particular author is probably not by him.

21. 'By a movement upward from the lowest depths.'

CHAPTER VIII.

The subject resumed—viz. the proper aims and characteristic directions and channels of the Nationalty. The Benefits of the National Church in time past. The present beneficial influences and workings of the same.

THE deep interest which, during the far larger portion of my life since early manhood I have attached to these convictions, has, I perceive, hurried me onwards as by the rush from the letting forth of accumulated waters by the sudden opening of the sluice gates. It is high time that I should return to my subject. And I have no better way of taking up the thread of my argument, than by re-stating my opinion, that our Eighth Henry would have acted in correspondence to the great principles of our constitution, if having restored the original balance on both sides, he had determined the nationalty to the following objects: 1st. To the maintenance of the Universities and the great liberal schools. 2ndly. To the maintenance of a pastor and schoolmaster in every parish. 3rdly. To the raising and keeping in repair of the churches, schools, &c., and, Lastly: To the maintenance of the proper, that is, the infirm, poor whether from age or sickness; one of the original purposes of the national Reserve being the alleviation of those evils, which in the best forms of worldly states must arise and must have been foreseen as arising from the institution of individual properties and primogeniture. If these duties were efficiently performed, and these purposes adequately fulfilled, the very increase of the population, (which would, however, by these very means have been prevented from becoming a vicious population,) would have more than counterbalanced those savings in the expenditure of the nationalty occasioned by the detachment of the practitioners of law, medicine, &c., from the national clergy. That this transfer of the national reserve from what had become national evils to its original and inherent purpose of national benefits, instead of the sacrilegious alienation which actually took place—that this was impracticable, is historically true: but no less true is it philosophically that this impracticability, arising wholly from moral causes—that is, from loose manners and corrupt principles—does not rescue this wholesale sacrilege from deserving the character of the first and deadliest wound inflicted on the constitution of the kingdom: which term constitution in the body politic, as in bodies natural, expresses not only what has been actually evolved, but likewise whatever is potentially contained in the seminal principle of the particular body, and would in its due time have appeared but for emasculation or disease. Other wounds, by which indeed the constitution of the nation has suffered, but which much more immediately concern the constitution of the church, we shall perhaps find another place to mention.

The mercantile and commercial class, in which I here comprise all the four classes that I have put in antithesis to the Landed Order, the guardian, and depository of the *Permanence* of the Realm, as more characteristically conspiring to the interests of its progression, the improvement and general freedom of the country—this class did as I have already remarked, in the earlier states of the constitution, exist but as in the bud. But during all this period of potential existence, or what we may call the minority of the burgess order, the National Church was the substitute for the most important national benefits resulting from the same. The National Church presented the only breathing hole of hope. The church alone relaxed the iron fate by which feudal dependency, primogeniture, and entail would otherwise have predestined every native of the realm to be lord or vassal. To the Church alone could the nation look for the benefits of existing knowledge, and for the means of future civilization. Lastly, let it never be forgotten, that under the fostering wing of the church, the class of free citizens and burgers were reared. To the feudal system we owe the *forms*, to the church the *substance*, of our liberty. We mention only two of many facts that would form the proof and comment of the above; first, the origin of towns and cities, in the privileges attached to the vicinity of churches and monasteries, and which preparing an asylum for the fugitive Vassal and oppressed Franklin, thus laid the first foundation of a class of freemen detached from the land. Secondly, the holy war, which the national clergy, in this instance faithful to their national duties, waged against slavery and villenage, and with such success, that in the reign of Charles II., the law which declared every native of the realm free by birth,[1] had merely to sanction an opus jam consummatum. Our Maker has distinguished man from the brute that perishes, by making hope first an instinct of his nature; and secondly, an indispensable condition of his moral and intellectual progression:

> "For every gift of noble origin
> Is breathed upon by Hope's perpetual breath."
> WORDSWORTH.[2]

But a natural instinct constitutes a right, as far as its gratification is compatible with the equal rights of others. And this principle we may expand, and apply to the idea of the National Church.

Among the primary ends of a STATE, (in that highest sense of the word, in which it is equivalent to the nation, considered as one body politic, and therefore includes the National Church), there are two, of which the National Church (according to its idea), is the especial and constitutional organ and means. The one is, to secure to the subjects of the realm generally, the hope, the chance, of bettering their own or their children's condition. And though during the last three or four centuries, the National church has found a most powerful surrogate and ally for the effectuation of this great purpose in her former wards and foster-children, *i.e.* in trade, commerce, free industry, and the arts—yet still the nationalty, under all defalcations, continues to feed the higher ranks by drawing up whatever is worthiest from below, and thus maintains the principle of Hope in the humblest families, while it secures the possessions of the rich and noble. This is one of the two ends.

The other is, to develope, in every native of the country, those faculties, and to provide for every native that knowledge and those attainments, which are necessary to qualify him for a member of the state, the free subject of a civilized realm. We do not mean those degrees of moral and intellectual cultivation which distinguish man from man in the same civilized society, much less those that separate the Christian from the this-worldian; but those only that constitute the civilized man in contra-distinction from the barbarian, the savage, and the animal.

I have now brought together all that seemed requisite to put the intelligent reader in full possession of (what I believe to be) the right Idea of the National Clergy, as an estate of the realm. But I cannot think my task finished without an attempt to rectify the too frequent false feeling on this subject, and to remove certain vulgar errors, errors, alas! not confined to those whom the world call the vulgar. Ma nel mondo non è se non volgo, says Machiavel.[3] I shall make no apology therefore, for interposing between the preceding statements, and the practical conclusion from them, the following paragraph, extracted from a work long out of print, and of such very limited circulation that I might have stolen from myself with little risk of detection, had it not been my wish to shew that the convictions expressed in the preceding pages, are not the offspring of the moment, brought forth for the present occasion; but an expansion of sentiments and principles publicly avowed in the year 1817.

Among [4] the numerous blessings of the English Constitution,[5] the introduction of an established Church makes an especial claim on the gratitude of scholars and philosophers; in England, at least, where the principles of Protestantism have conspired with the freedom of the government to double all its salutary powers by the removal of its abuses.

59

That the maxims of a pure morality, and those sublime truths of the divine unity and attributes, which a Plato found hard to learn, and more difficult to reveal; that these should have become the almost hereditary property of childhood and poverty, of the hovel and the workshop; that even to the unlettered they sound as *common place*; this is a phenomenon which must withhold all but minds of the most vulgar cast from undervaluing the services even of the pulpit and the reading desk. Yet he who should *confine* the efficiency of an Established Church to these, can hardly be placed in a much higher rank of intellect. That to every parish throughout the kingdom there is transplanted a germ of civilization: that in the remotest villages there is a nucleus, round which the capabilities of the place may crystallise and brighten; a model sufficiently superior to excite, yet sufficiently near to encourage and facilitate, imitation; *this* unobtrusive, continuous agency of a Protestant Church Establishment, *this* it is, which the patriot, and the philanthropist, who would fain unite the love of peace with the faith in the progressive amelioration of mankind, cannot estimate at too high a price—" It cannot be valued with the gold of Ophir, with the precious onyx, or the sapphire. No mention shall be made of coral or of pearls: for the price of wisdom is above rubies." [6]—The clergyman is with his parishoners and among them; he is neither in the cloistered cell, nor in the wilderness, but a neighbour and family-man, whose education and rank admit him to the mansion of the rich landholder, while his duties make him the frequent visiter of the farmhouse and the cottage. He is, or he may become, connected with the families of his parish or its vicinity by marriage. And among the instances of the blindness or at best of the short-sightedness, which it is the nature of cupidity to inflict, I know few more striking, than the clamours of the farmers against church property. Whatever was not paid to the clergymen would inevitably at the next lease be paid to the landholder, while, as the case at present stands, the revenues of the church are in some sort the reversionary property of every family that may have a member educated for the church, or a daughter that may marry a clergyman. Instead of being *fore closed* and immoveable, it is, in fact, the only species of landed property that is essentially moving and circulative. That there exist no inconveniencies, who will pretend to assert? But I have yet to expect the proof, that the inconveniences are greater in this than in any other species; or that either the farmers or the clergy would be benefited by forcing the latter to become either *trullibers* [7] or salaried *placemen*. Nay, I do not hesitate to declare my firm persuasion that whatever *reason* of discontent the farmers may assign, the true *cause* is that they may cheat the *Parson* but cannot cheat the steward; and they are disappointed if they should have been able to withold only two pounds less than the legal claim, having expected to withhold five.

1. 'The Author means the Act passed at the Restoration, 12 C.II.c.24. "And these encroachments grew to be so universal, that when tenure in villenage was virtually abolished (though copyholds were preserved) by the statute of Charles II., there was hardly a pure villein left in the nation," &c., Blackstone II. c. 6. 96' (H.N.C.).
2. From *Sonnets dedicated to National Independence and Liberty*, XX.
3. 'But in the world there is nothing that is not vulgar'; *The Prince*, XVIII.
4. The passage from here to the end of the chapter is from *BL* (Everyman edition, pp. 129–30).
5. 'English Constitution,' all editions; 'Christianity', *BL*.
6. Job xxviii. 16 & 18.
7. Trulliber is the curate in *Joseph Andrews* who, no doubt as a result of the penury of his living, has devoted himself to farming and to laying up treasure on earth.

CHAPTER IX.

Practical Conclusion: What unfits; and what excludes from the National Church.

THE clerisy, or National Church, being an estate of the realm, the Church and State with the king as the sovereign head of both constituting the Body Politic, the State in the large sense of the word, or the NATION dynamically considered (ἐν δυνάμει κατὰ πνεῦμα,[1] *i.e.* as an *ideal*, but not the less *actual* and abiding, unity); and in like manner, the Nationalty being one of the two constitutional modes or species, of which the common wealth of the nation consists; it follows by the immediate consequence, that of the qualifications for the trusteeship, absolutely to be required of the order collectively, and of every individual person as the conditions of his admission into this order, and of his liability to the usufruct or life-interest of any part or parcel of the Nationalty, the first and most indispensable qualification and pre-condition, that without which all others are null and void,— is that the National Clergy, and every member of the same from the highest to the lowest, shall be fully and exclusively citizens of the State, neither acknowledging the authority, nor within the influence of any other State in the world—full and undistracted subjects of this kingdom, and in no capacity, and under no pretences, owning any other earthly sovereign or visible head but the king, in whom alone the majesty of the nation is *apparent*, and by whom alone the unity of the nation in will and in deed is symbolically expressed and impersonated.

The full extent of this first and absolutely necessary qualification will be best seen in stating the contrary, that is, the absolute disqualifications, the existence of which in any individual, and in any class or order of men, constitutionally incapacitates such individual and class or order from being inducted into the National Trust: and this on a principle so vitally concerning the health and integrity of the body politic, as to render the voluntary transfer of the nationalty, whole or part, direct or indirect, to an order notoriously thus disqualified, a foul treason against the most fundamental rights and interests of the realm, and of all classes of its citizens and free subjects, the individuals of the very order itself, *as* citizens and subjects, not excepted. Now there are two things, and but two, which evidently and predeterminably disqualify for this great trust: the first absolutely, and the second, which in its collective operation, and as an attribute of the whole class, would, of itself, constitute the greatest possible unfitness for the proper ends and purposes of the National Church, as explained and specified in the preceding paragraphs, and the heaviest drawback from the civilizing influence of the National Clergy in their pastoral and parochial character—the second, I say, by implying the former, becomes likewise an *absolute* ground of disqualification. It is scarcely necessary to add, what the reader will have anticipated, that the first absolute disqualification is allegiance to a foreign power: the second, the abjuration—under the command and authority of this power, and as by the rule of their order its professed Lieges (Alligati)—of that bond, which more than all other ties connects the citizen with his country; which beyond all other securities affords the surest pledge to the state for the fealty of its citizens, and that which (when the rule is applied to any body or class of men, under whatever name united, where the number is sufficiently great to neutralize the accidents of individual temperament and circumstances) enables the State to calculate on their constant adhesion to its interests, and to rely on their faith and singleness of heart in the due execution of whatever public or national trust might be assigned to them.

But we shall, perhaps, express the nature of this security more adequately by the negative. The Marriage Tie is a Bond the preclusion of which by an antecedent obligation, that overrules the accidents of individual character and is common to the whole order, deprives the State of a security with which it cannot dispense. I will not say, that it is a security which the State may rightfully demand of all its adult citizens, competently circumstanced, by positive enactment: though I might shelter the position under the authority of the great Publicists and State-Lawyers of the Augustan Age, who, in the Lex Julia Papia,[2] enforced anew a principle common to the old Roman Constitution with that of Sparta.[3] But without the least fear of confutation, though in the full foresight of vehement contradiction, I do assert, that the State may rightfully demand of any number of its subjects united in one body or order the *absence* of all customs, initiative vows, covenants and by-laws in that order, precluding the members of the said body collectively and individually from affording this security. In strictness of principle, I might here conclude the sentence—though as it now stands it would involve the assertion of a right in the state to suppress any order confederated under laws so anti-civic. But I am no friend to any rights that can be disjoined from the *duty* of enforcing them. I therefore at once confine and complete the sentence thus:—The State not only possesses the right of demanding, but is in duty bound to demand, the above as a *necessary condition* of its entrusting to any order of men, and to any individual as a member of a known order, the titles, functions, and investments of the *National* Church.

But if any doubt could attach to the proposition, whether thus stated or in the perfectly equivalent *Converse, i.e.* that the existence and known enforcement of the injunction or prohibitory by-law, before described, in any Order or Incorporation constitutes an *a priori* disqualification for the Trusteeship of the Nationalty, and an insuperable obstacle to the establishment of such an order, or of any members of the same as a National Clergy—such doubt would be removed, as soon as the fact of this injunction, or vow exacted and given, or whatever else it may be, by which the members of the Order, collectively and as such, incapacitate themselves from affording this security for their full, faithful, and unbiassed application of a *National* Trust to its proper and national purposes, is found in conjunction with, and aggravated by, the three following circumstances. First, that this incapacitation originates in, and forms part of, the allegiance of the order to a foreign Sovereignty: Secondly, that it is notorious, that the Canon or Prescript, on which it is grounded,[4] was first enforced on the secular clergy universally, after long and obstinate reluctation on their side, and on that of their natural sovereigns in the several realms, to which as subjects they belonged; and that it is still retained in force, and its revocation inflexibly refused, as the direct and only adequate means of *supporting* that usurped and foreign Sovereignty, and of securing by virtue of the expatriating and insulating effect of its operation, the devotion, and allegiance of the order * to their visible Head, and Sovereign. And thirdly, that the operation of the interdict precludes one of the most constant and influencive ways and means of promoting the great paramount end of a National Church, the progressive civilization of the community. Emollit mores nec sinit esse feros.[5]

And now let me conclude these preparatory Notices by compressing the sum and substance of my argument into this one sentence. Though many things may detract from the comparative fitness of individuals, or of particular classes, for the Trust and Functions of the NATIONALTY, there are only two *absolute* Disqualifications: and these are, Allegiance to a Foreign Power, or the Acknowledgement of any other visible HEAD OF THE CHURCH, but our Sovereign Lord the King: and compulsory celibacy in connection with, and in dependence on, a foreign and extra-national head.

* For the fullest and ablest exposition of this point, I refer to the Reverend Blanco White's "Practical and Internal Evidence," [6] and to that admirable work, "Riforma d'Italia," [7] written by a professed and apparently sincere Catholic, a work which well merits translation. I know no work so well fitted to soften the prejudices against the theoretical doctrines of the Latin Church, and to deepen our reprobation of what it actually and practically *is*, in all countries where the expediency of keeping up appearances, as in Protestant neighbourhoods, does not operate.

1. 'In power according to the Spirit'; like many phrases Pauline in inspiration, this one remains Greek even after being translated. For ἐν δυνάμει, see 1 Corinthians iv. 20, and 1 Thessalonians i, 5, where the phrase is used in contrast with ἐν λόγῳ, 'in word'.

2. 'Lex Papia Poppaea', 3rd edition (more correctly). 'A.U.C. 762.—"sentries were set over us, and (by the Papia Poppaea Law) lured on by rewards; so that, if a man shirked the privileges of paternity, the state, as universal parent, might step into the vacant inheritance." Tacitus, *Annals* III, 28' (H.N.C., who gives the quotation in Latin).

3. 'Marriage was almost universal among the citizens [of Sparta], enforced by general opinion at least, if not by law.' Grote, *History of Greece*, II. 2. vi.

4. An enactment of the First Lateran Council (Can. XXI) in 1123.

5. 'It softens the manners, and does not permit them to be brutal.' Ovid, *Epistulae ex Ponto*, II. ix. 48.

6. Joseph Blanco White (1775–1841), a convert to Anglicanism from the Spanish Catholic priesthood, published his *Practical and Internal Evidences Against Catholicism* in 1825. It was much admired by Southey and by Coleridge and both men became close friends of White.

7. Anonymous, but by Carlo Antonio Pilati, Venice 1767.

CHAPTER X.

On the King and the Nation.

A TREATISE? why, the subjects might, I own, excite some apprehension of the sort. But it will be found like sundry Greek Treatises among the tinder-rolls of Herculaneum, with titles of as large promise, somewhat largely and irregularly abbreviated in the process of unrolling. In fact, neither my purpose nor my limits permit more than a few hints, that may prepare the reader for some of the positions assumed in the second part of this volume.

Of the King with the two Houses of Parliament, as constituting the STATE (in the special and antithetic sense of the word) we have already spoken: and it remains only to determine the proper and legitimate objects of its superintendence and control. On what is the power of the State rightfully exercised? Now, I am not arguing in a court of law; and my purpose would be grievously misunderstood if what I say should be taken as intended for an assertion of the *fact*. Neither of facts, nor of statutory and demandable rights do I speak; but exclusively of the STATE according to the *idea*. And, in accordance with the *idea* of the State, I do not hesitate to answer, that the legitimate objects of its power comprise all the interests and concerns of the PROPRIETAGE, both landed and personal, and whether inheritably vested in the lineage or in the individual citizen; and these alone. Even in the lives and limbs of the lieges, the King, as the head and arm of the State, has an interest of property: and in any trespass against them the King appears as plaintiff.

The chief object, for which men who from the beginning existed as a social bond, first formed themselves into a *State*, and on the social superinduced the political relation, was not the protection of their lives but of their property. The natural man is too proud an animal to admit that he needs any other protection for his life than his own courage and that of his clan can bestow. Where the nature of the soil and climate has precluded all property but personal, and admitted that only in its simplest forms, as in Greenland for instance—there men remain in the domestic state and form neighbourhoods, not governments. And in North America, the chiefs appear to exercise government in those tribes only which possess individual landed property. Among the rest the chief is the general, a leader in war; not a magistrate. To property and to its necessary inequalities must be referred all human laws, that would not be laws without and independent of any conventional enactment: *i.e.* all State-legislation.—FRIEND, vol i. 351.

Next comes the King, as the Head of the National Church, or Clerisy, and the Protector and Supreme Trustee of the NATIONALTY: the power of the same in relation to its proper objects being exercised by the King and the Houses of Convocation, of which, as before of the State, the King is the head and arm. And here if it had been my purpose to enter at once on the development of this position, together with the conclusions to be drawn from it, I should need with increased earnestness remind the reader, that I am neither describing what the National Church now is, nor determining what it ought to be. My statements respect the idea alone, as deduced from its original purpose and ultimate aim: and of the *idea* only must my assertions be understood. But the full exposition of this point is not necessary for the appreciation of the late Bill which is the subject of the following part of the volume. It belongs indeed to the chapter with which I had intended to conclude this volume, and which, should my health permit, and the circumstances warrant it, it is still my intention to let follow the present work—namely, my humble contribution towards an answer to the question, What is to be done now? For the present, therefore, it will be sufficient, if I recal to the reader's recollection, that formerly the National Clerisy, in the two Houses of Convocation duly assembled and represented, taxed themselves.[1] But as to the proper objects, on which the authority of the convocation with the King as its head was to be exercised—these the reader will himself without difficulty decypher by referring to what has been already said respecting the proper and distinguishing ends and purposes of a National Church.

I pass, therefore, at once to the relations of the Nation, or the State in the larger sense of the word, to the State especially so named, and to the Crown. And on this subject again I shall confine myself to a few important, yet, I trust, not common nor obvious, remarks respecting the conditions requisite or especially favorable to the health and vigor of the realm. From these again I separate those, the nature and importance of which cannot be adequately exhibited but by adverting to the consequences which have followed their neglect or inobservance, reserving them for another place: while for the present occasion I select two only; but these, I dare believe, not unworthy the name of Political Principles, or *Maxims*, *i.e.* regulæ quæ inter *maximas* numerari merentur.[2] And both of them forcibly confirm and exemplify a remark, often and in various ways suggested to my mind, that with, perhaps, one * exception, it would be difficult in the whole compass of language, to find a metaphor so commensurate, so pregnant, or suggesting so many points of elucidation, as that of *Body Politic*, as the exponent of a State or Realm. I admire, as little as you do, the many-jointed similitudes of Flavel,[4] and other finders of moral and spiritual meanings in the works of Art and Nature, where the proportion of the likeness to the difference not seldom reminds us of the celebrated comparison of the Morning Twilight to a Boiled Lobster.[5] But the correspondence between the Body Politic to the Body Natural holds even in the detail of application. Let it not however be supposed, that I expect to derive any proof of my positions from this analogy. My object in thus prefacing them is answered, if I have shown cause for the use of the

---

* That namely of the WORD (*Gosp. of John*, i. 1.) for the Divine Alterity; the Deus Alter et idem of Philo; [3] *Deitas Objectiva.*

physiological terms by which I have sought to render my meaning intelligible.

The first condition then required, in order to a sound constitution of the Body Politic, is a due proportion of the free and permeative life and energy of the Nation to the organized powers brought within containing channels. What those vital forces that seem to bear an analogy to the imponderable agents, magnetic, or galvanic, in bodies inorganic, if indeed, they are not the same in a higher energy and under a different law of action—what these, I say, are in the living body in distinction from the fluids in the glands and vessels—the same, or at least a like relation, do the indeterminable, but yet actual influences of intellect, information, prevailing principles and tendencies, (to which we must add the influence of property, or income, where it exists without right of suffrage attached thereto), hold to the regular, definite, and legally recognised Powers, in the Body Politic. But as no simile runs on all four legs (*nihil simile est idem*),[6] so here the difference in respect of the Body Politic is, that in sundry instances the former, *i.e.* the permeative, species of force is capable of being converted into the latter, of being as it were organized and rendered a part of the vascular system, by attaching a measured and determinate political right, or privilege thereto.

What the exact proportion, however, of the two kinds of force should be, it is impossible to predetermine. But the existence of a disproportion is sure to be detected, sooner or later, by the effects. Thus: the ancient Greek democracies, the *hot-beds* of Art, Science, Genius, and Civilization, fell into dissolution from the excess of the former, the permeative power deranging the functions, and by explosions shattering the organic structures, they should have enlivened. On the contrary, the Republic of Venice fell by the contrary extremes. All political power was confined to the determinate vessels, and these becoming more and more rigid, even to an ossification of the arteries, the State, in which the people were nothing, lost all power of resistance ad extra.

Under this head, in short, there are three possible sorts of malformation to be noticed, namely,—The adjunction or concession of direct political power to *personal* force and influence, whether physical or intellectual, existing in classes or aggregates of individuals, without those fixed or tangible possessions, freehold, copyhold, or leasehold, in land, house, or stock. The power resulting from the acquisition of knowledge or skill, and from the superior developement of the understanding is, doubtless, of a far nobler kind than mere physical strength and fierceness, the one being *peculiar* to the animal *Man*, the other common to him with the Bear, the Buffalo, and the Mastiff. And if superior Talents, and the mere possession of knowledges, such as can be learnt at Mechanics' Institutions, were regularly accompanied with a Will in harmony with the Reason, and a consequent subordination of the appetites and passions to the ultimate ends of our Being: if intellectual gifts and attainments were infallible signs of wisdom and goodness in the same proportion, and the knowing, clever, and *talented* (a vile word!) were always *rational*; if the mere facts of science conferred or superseded the soft'ning humanizing influences of the moral world, that habitual presence of the beautiful or the seemly, and that exemption from all familiarity with the gross, the mean, and the disorderly, whether in look or language, or in the surrounding objects, in which the main efficacy of a liberal education consists; and if, lastly, these acquirements and powers of the understanding could be shared equally by the whole class, and did not, as by a necessity of nature they ever must do, fall to the lot of two or three in each several group, club, or neighbourhood;—then, indeed, by an enlargement of the Chinese system, political power might not unwisely be conferred as the honorarium or privilege on having passed through all the forms in the National Schools, without the security of political ties, without those fastenings and radical fibres of a collective and registrable property, by which the Citizen inheres in and belongs to the Commonwealth, as a constituent part either of the Proprietage, or of the Nationalty; either of the State, or of the National Church. But as the contrary of all these suppositions may be more safely assumed, the practical conclusion will be—not that the requisite means of intellectual developement and growth should be withheld from any native of the soil, which it was at all times wicked to wish, and which it would be now silly to attempt; but—that the gifts of the understanding, whether the boon of a genial nature, or the reward of more persistent application, should be allowed fair play in the acquiring of that proprietorship, to which a certain portion of political power belongs, as its proper function. For in this way there is at least a strong probability, that intellectual power will be armed with political power, only where it has previously been combined with and guarded by the moral qualities of prudence, industry, and self-control. And this is the first of the three kinds of mal-organization in a state: viz. direct political power without cognizable possession.

The second is: the exclusion of any class or numerous body of individuals, who have notoriously risen into possession, and the influence inevitably connected with known possession, under pretence of impediments that do not directly or essentially affect the character of the individuals as citizens, or absolutely disqualify them for the performance of civic duties. Imperfect, yet oppressive, and irritating ligatures that peril the trunk, whose circulating current they would withhold, even more than the limb which they would fain excommunicate!

The third and last is: a gross incorrespondency of the proportion of the antagonist interests of the Body Politic in the representative body—*i.e.* (in relation to our own country,) in the two Houses of Parliament—to the actual proportion of the same interests, and of the public influence exerted by the same in the Nation at large. Whether in consequence of the gradual revolution which has transferred to the Magnates of the Landed Interest so large a portion of that Borough Representation which was to have been its counterbalance; [7] whether the same causes which have deranged the equilibrium of the Landed and the * Monied Interests in the Legislation, have not likewise

* *Moniyed*, used arbitrarily, as in preceding pages the words, *Personal* and *Independent*, from my inability to find any one self-interpreting word, that would serve for the generic name of the four

deranged the balance between the two unequal divisions of the Landed Interest itself, viz., the Major Barons, or great Land-owners, with or without title, and the great body of the Agricultural Community, and thus given [9] to the real or imagined interests of the comparatively few, the imposing name of the

---

classes, on which I have stated the Interest of *Progression* more especially to depend, and with it the Freedom which is the indispensable *condition* and propelling force of all national progress: even as the Counter-pole, the other great Interest of the Body Politic, its *Permanency*, is more especially committed to the Landed Order, as its natural Guardian and Depository. I have therefore had recourse to the convenient figure of speech, by which a conspicuous part or feature of a subject is used to express the whole; and the reader will be so good as to understand, that the Moniyed Order in this place comprehends and stands for, the Commercial, Manufacturing, Distributive, and Professional classes of the Community.

Only a few days ago, an accident placed in my hand a work of which, from my very limited opportunities of seeing new publications, I had never before heard. Mr. CRAWFURD's History of the Indian Archipelago [8]—the work of a wise as well as of an able and well-informed man! Need I add, that it was no ordinary gratification to find, that in respect of certain prominent positions, maintained in this volume, I had unconsciously been fighting behind the shield of one whom I deem it an honour to follow. But the sheets containing the passages, having been printed off, I avail myself of this note, to insert the sentences from Mr. Crawfurd's History, rather than to lose the confirmation which a coincidence with so high an authority has produced on my own mind, and the additional weight which my sentiments, will receive in the judgment of others. The first of the two Extracts the reader will consider as annexed to pp. 17-18 of this volume; the second to the paragraph on the protection of property, as the end chiefly proposed in the formation of a fixed government, quoted from a work of my own, (viz. *The Friend*), published ten or eleven years before the appearance of Mr. Crawfurd's History, which I notice in the work to give the principle in question that probability of its being grounded in fact, which is derived from the agreement of two independent minds. The first extract, Mr. Crawfurd introduces by the remark, that the possession

Interest of the whole—the landed Interest!—these are questions, to which the obdurate adherence to the jail-crowding Game Laws, (which during the reading of our Church Litany, I have sometimes been tempted to include, by a sort of *sub intellige*,[10] in the petitions—"from envy, hatred, and malice, and all uncharitableness; from battle, murder, and sudden death, Good Lord, deliver us!") to which the Corn Laws, the exclusion of the produce of our own colonies from our distilleries, &c., during the war, against the earnest recommendation of the government, the retention of the Statutes against Usury,[11] and other points, of minor importance or of less safe handling, may seem at a first view to suggest an answer in the affirmative; but which, for reasons before assigned, I shall leave unresolved, content if only I have made the Principle itself intelligible.

The following anecdote, for I have no means of ascertaining its truth, and no warrant to offer for its accuracy, I give not as a fact in proof of an overbalance of the Landed Interest, but as an indistinctly remembered hearsay, in elucidation of what is meant by the words. Some eighteen or twenty years ago— for so long I think it must have been, since the circumstance was

---

of wealth, derived from a fertile soil, encouraged the progress of absolute power in Java. He then proceeds—

EXTRACT I.

The devotion of a people to agricultural industry, by rendering themselves more tame, and their property more tangible, went still farther towards it: *for wherever Agriculture is the principal pursuit, there it may certainly be reckoned, that the People will be found living under an absolute government.*

HISTORY OF THE INDIAN ARCHIPELAGO: vol. iii. p. 24.

EXTRACT II.

In cases of murder, no distinction is made (*i.e. in the Ancient Laws of the Indian Islanders*), between wilful murder and chance medley. *It is the Loss, which the family or tribe sustains, that is considered, and the pecuniary compensation was calculated to make up that loss.*

DITTO, DITTO, p. 123.

first related to me—my illustrious (alas! I must add, I fear, my *late*) friend, Sir Humphrey Davy, at Sir Joseph Banks's request,[12] analysed a portion of an East Indian import, known by the names of cutch, and Terra Japonica;[13] but which he ascertained to be a vegetable extract, consisting almost wholly of pure *tannin*: and further trials, with less pure specimens, still led to the conclusion, that the average product would be seven parts in ten of the tanning principle. This discovery was * communicated to the trade; and on inquiry made at the India House, it was found that this cutch could be prepared in large

---

* And, (if I recollect right, though it was not from him, that I received the anecdote) by a friend of Sir Humphrey's, whom I am proud to think *my* friend likewise, and by an elder claim.[14]—A man whom I have seen now in his harvest field, or the market, now in a committee-room, with the Rickmans and Ricardos of the age; at another time with Davy, Woolaston, and the Wedgewoods;[15] now with Wordsworth, Southey, and other friends not unheard of in the republic of letters; now in the drawing-rooms of the rich and the noble, and now presiding at the annual dinner of a Village Benefit Society; and in each seeming to be in the very place he was intended for, and taking the part to which his tastes, talents, and attainments, gave him an admitted right. And yet this is not the most remarkable, not the individualising trait of our friend's character. It is almost overlooked in the originality and raciness of his intellect; in the life, freshness and practical value of his remarks and notices, truths plucked as they are growing, and delivered to you with the dew on them, the fair earnings of an observing eye, armed and kept on the watch by thought and meditation; and above all, in the integrity, *i.e. entireness* of his being, (*integrum et sine cerâ vas*),[16] the steadiness of his attachments, and the activity and persistency of a benevolence, which so graciously presses a warm temper into the service of a yet warmer heart, and so lights up the little flaws and imperfections, incident to humanity in its choicest specimens, that were their removal at the option of his friends, (and few have, or deserve to have so many!) not a man among them but would vote for leaving him as he is.

This is a note *digressive*; but, as the height of the offence is, that the Garnish is too good for the Dish, I shall confine my apology to a confession of the fault.   S. T. C.

quantities, and imported at a price which, after an ample profit to the importers, it would very well answer the purposes of the tanners to give. The trade itself, too, was likely to be greatly benefitted and enlarged by being rendered less dependent on particular situations; while the reduction of the price at which it could be offered to the foreign consumer, acting in conjunction with the universally admitted superiority of the English leather, might be reasonably calculated on as enabling us to undersell our foreign rivals in their own markets. Accordingly, an offer was made, on the part of the principal persons interested in the leather trade, to purchase, at any price below the sum that had been stated to them as the highest, or extreme price, as large a quantity as it was probable that the Company would find it feasible or convenient to import in the first instance. Well! the ships went out, and the ships returned, again and again: and no increase in the amount of the said desideratum appearing among the imports, enough only being imported to meet the former demand of the druggists, and (it is whispered) of certain ingenious transmuters of Bohea into Hyson [17]—my memory does not enable me to determine whether the inquiry into the occasion of this disappointment was *made*, or whether it was anticipated, by a discovery that it would be useless. But it *was generally understood*, that the Tanners had not been the only persons, whose attention had been drawn to the qualities of the article, and the consequences of its importation; and that a very intelligible hint had been given to persons of known influence in Leadenhall-street, that in case of any such importation being allowed, the East-India Company must not expect any support from the *Landed Interest* in parliament, at the next renewal, or motion for the renewal of their Charter. The East India Company might reduce the price of Bark, one half, or more: and the British Navy, and the grandsons of our present Senators, might thank them for thousands and myriads of noble oaks, left unstript in consequence—this may be true; but no less true is it, that the Free Merchants would soon reduce the price of good Tea, in the same proportion, and monopolists ought to have a feeling for each other.

1. This right was surrendered by Convocation in 1664.
2. 'Rules worthy to be numbered among the most important.'
3. The 'God who is at once other than he is, and the same'; Philo (*c.* 25 B.C.–*c.* A.D. 50.), Jewish philosopher and theologian, developed an idea of God at once absolutely abstract, as logic required him to be, and personal, as an embodiment of the moral qualities valued by Jewish piety.
4. John Flavel (1630?–91), Presbyterian divine and voluminous writer, a selection of whose work had appeared in 1823.
5. Butler, *Hudibras*, Canto II. 1. 31.
6. 'Nothing similar is the same.'
7. Coleridge refers to (a) the rotten-borough system, and (b) the alliance between the middle and propertied classes, and the Tory gentry, against the great Whig landowners, on which the long Tory supremacy of the first decades of the nineteenth century was based.
8. John Crawfurd (1783–1868), orientalist. The *History* appeared in 1820.
9. 'giving', 2nd edition, corrected in 3rd edition.
10. Something which is supplied in thought, or understood in addition.
11. At various times during the French Wars the distilleries in Britain and Ireland were stopped by Parliament from using grain. The statutes against usury limited the amount of interest that might be charged on a loan. Brougham argued for their repeal in 1816, and in the following year and in 1819 bills to repeal the statutes were introduced and withdrawn. The statutes were repealed (in part) in 1833, and finally in 1854.
12. Sir Joseph Banks (1743–1820), President of the Royal Society.
13. An astringent substance obtained from the wood of the *acacia catecha*, and containing up to fifty-five per cent tannin; when first brought to England it was thought to be an earth, and named *terra japonica*.
14. Thomas Poole (1765–1837), lifelong friend and benefactor of Coleridge.
15. William Hyde Woollaston (1766–1828), chemist and physicist; John Rickman (1771–1840), statistician, who devised the methods employed in the first four decennial censuses (1801–41).
16. 'A vessel whole and clean' (lit., 'and without wax'). *Sincerus* (clean, pure) was originally thought to be derived from *sine cera*

on the argument that pure honey was free of wax; see Horace, *Epistles*, I. ii. 54, and *Satires*, I. iii. 56, and the scholium to *Epodes*, ii, 15.

17. 'Bohea' is a name given originally to the finest of black teas from the Wu-i Hills in North Fuhkien. By Coleridge's time, however, it was the worst—because the last—crop of the summer that was called 'bohea'. 'Hyson' is a coarse green tea, but 'young Hyson', to which he no doubt refers, is of fine quality. Presumably the tannin in the cutch would have improved the strength, if nothing else, of the tea to which it was added.

CHAPTER XI.

The relations of the potential to the actual. The omnipotence of Parliament: of what kind.

So much, in explanation of the first of the two *Conditions* of the health and vigour of a Body Politic: and far more, I must confess, than I had myself reckoned on. I will endeavour to indemnify the reader, by despatching the second in a few sentences, which could not so easily have been accomplished, but for the explanations given in the preceding paragraphs. For as we have found the first condition in the due proportion of the free and permeative Life of the State to the Powers organized, and severally determined by their appropriate and containing, or conducting nerves, or vessels; the Second Condition is—

A due proportion of the *potential* (latent, dormant) to the *actual* Power. In the first Condition, both Powers alike are awake and in act. The Balance is produced by the *polarization* of the Actual Power, *i.e.* the opposition of the Actual Power organized, to the Actual Power free and permeating the organs. In the Second, the Actual Power, *in toto*, is opposed to the Potential. It has been frequently and truly observed, that in England, where the ground plan, the skeleton, as it were, of the government is a monarchy, at once buttressed and limited by the Aristocracy, (the assertions of its popular character finding a better support in the harangues and theories of popular men, than in state-documents and the records of clear History), a far greater degree of liberty is, and long has been enjoyed, than ever existed in the ostensibly freest, that is, most democratic, Commonwealths of ancient or of modern times—greater, indeed, and with a more decisive predominance of the Spirit of Freedom, than the wisest and most philanthropic statesmen of antiquity, or than the great Commonwealth's-men, the stars of that narrow interspace of blue sky between the black clouds of the first and second Charles's reigns) believed compatible, the one with the safety of the State, the other with the interests of Morality.

Yes! for little less than a century and a half Englishmen have collectively, and individually, lived and acted with fewer restraints on their free-agency, than the citizens of any known * Republic, past or present. The fact is certain. It has been often boasted of, but never, I think, clearly explained. The solution of the phenomenon must, it is obvious, be sought for in the combination of circumstances, to which we owe the insular privilege of a self-evolving Constitution: and the following will, I think, be found the main cause of the fact in question. Extremes meet—an adage of inexhaustible exemplification. A democratic Republic and an Absolute Monarchy agree in this; that in both alike, the Nation, or People, delegates its whole power. Nothing is left obscure, nothing suffered to remain in the Idea, unevolved and only acknowledged as an existing, yet interminable Right. A Constitution such states can scarcely be said to possess. The whole Will of the Body Politic is in act at every moment. But in the Constitution of England according to the Idea, (which in this instance has demonstrated its actuality by its practical influence, and this too though counter-worked by fashionable errors and maxims, that left their validity behind in the Law-Courts, from which they were borrowed)

---

* It will be thought, perhaps, that the United States of North America should have been excepted. But the identity of Stock, Language, Customs, Manners and Laws scarcely allows us to consider this an exception: even tho' it were quite certain both that it is and that it will continue such. It was, at all events, a remark worth remembering, which I once heard from a Traveller (a prejudiced one I must admit) that where every man may take liberties, there is little Liberty for any man—or, that where every man takes liberties, no man can enjoy any.[1]

the Nation has delegated its power, not without measure and circumscription, whether in respect of the duration of the Trust, or of the particular interests entrusted.

The Omnipotence of Parliament, in the mouth of a lawyer, and understood exclusively of the restraints and remedies within the competence of our Law-courts, is objectionable only as bombast. It is but a puffing pompous way of stating a plain matter of fact. Yet in the times preceding the Restoration, even this was not universally admitted. And it is not without a fair show of reason, that the shrewd and learned author of "THE ROYALIST'S DEFENCE;" printed in the year 1648,[2] (a tract of 172 pages, small quarto, from which I now transcribe) thus sums up his argument and evidences:

"Upon the whole matter clear it is, the Parliament itself (that is, the King, the Lords, and Commons) although unanimously consenting, are *not boundless*: the Judges of the Realm by the *fundamental* Law of *England* have power to determine which Acts of Parliament are binding and which void.' p. 48.—That a unanimous declaration of the Judges of the realm, that any given Act of Parliament was against right reason and the fundamental law of the land (*i.e.* the Constitution of the realm), render such Act null and void, was a principle that did not want defenders among the lawyers of elder times. And in a state of society in which the competently informed and influencive members of the community, (the National Clerisy not included), scarcely perhaps trebled the number of the members of the two Houses, and Parliaments were so often tumultuary congresses of a victorious party rather than representatives of the State, the right and Power here asserted might have been wisely vested in the Judges of the realm: and with at least equal wisdom, under change of circumstances, has the right been suffered to fall into abeyance. Therefore let the potency of Parliament be that highest and uttermost, beyond which a court of Law looketh not: and within the sphere of the Courts quicquid Rex cum Parliamento voluit, *Fatum* sit!" [3]

But if the strutting phrase be taken, as from sundry recent speeches respecting the fundamental institutions of the realm it may be reasonably inferred, that it has been taken, *i.e.* absolutely, and in reference, not to our Courts of Law exclusively, but to the Nation, to England with all her venerable heir-looms, and with all her germs of reversionary wealth—thus used and understood, the Omnipotence of Parliament is an hyperbole, that would contain mischief in it, were it only that it tends to provoke a detailed analysis of the materials of the joint-stock company, to which so terrific an attribute belongs, and the competence of the shareholders in this earthly omnipotence to exercise the same. And on this head the observations and descriptive statements given in Chap. v. of the old tract, just cited, retain all their force; or if any have fallen off, their place has been abundantly filled up by new growths. The degree and sort of knowledge, talent, probity, and prescience, which it would be only too easy, were it not too invidious, to prove from acts and measures presented by the history of the last half century, are but *scant measure* even when exerted within the sphere and circumscription of the constitution, and on the matters properly and peculiarly appertaining to the State according to the idea [4]—this portion of moral and mental endowment placed by the side of the plusquam-gigantic height and amplitude of power, implied in the unqualified use of the phrase, Omnipotence of Parliament, and with its dwarfdom exaggerated by the contrast, would threaten to distort the countenance of truth itself with the sardonic laugh of irony.[*]

The non-resistance of successive generations has ever been, and with evident reason, deemed equivalent to a tacit consent,

[*] I have not in my possession the morning paper in which I read it, or I should with great pleasure transcribe an admirable passage from the present King of Sweden's Address to the STORTHING, *i.e.* Parliament of Norway, on the necessary limits of Parliamentary Power, consistently with the existence of a CONSTITUTION. But I can with confidence refer the reader to the speech, as worthy of an Alfred. Every thing indeed that I have heard or read of this sovereign, has contributed to the impression on my mind, that he is a good and wise man, and worthy to be the king of a virtuous people, the purest specimen of the Gothic race.

on the part of the nation, and as finally legitimating the act thus acquiesced in, however great the dereliction of principle, and breach of trust, the original enactment may have been. I hope, therefore, that without offence I may venture to designate the Septennial Act,[5] as an act of usurpation, tenfold more dangerous to the true Liberty of the Nation, than the pretext for the measure, viz. the apprehended Jacobite leaven from a new election, was at all likely to have proved: and I repeat the conviction, I have expressed in reference to the practical suppression of the CONVOCATION,[6] that no great principle was ever invaded or trampled on, that did not sooner or later avenge itself on the country, and even on the governing classes themselves, by the consequences of the precedent. The statesmen who has not learnt this from history, has missed its most valuable result, and might in my opinion as profitably, and far more delightfully have devoted his hours of study to Sir Walter Scott's Novels.*

But I must draw in my reins. Neither my limits permit, nor does my present purpose require that I should do more than exemplify the limitation resulting from that latent or *potential* Power, a due proportion of which to the actual powers I have stated as the second condition of the health and vigor of a body politic, by an instance bearing directly on the measure, which in the following section I am to aid in appreciating, and which was the occasion of the whole work. The principle itself, which, as not contained within the rule and compass of law, its practical manifestations being indeterminable and inappreciable *a priori*, and then only to be recorded as having manifested itself, when the predisposing causes and the enduring effects prove the unific mind and energy of the nation to have been in travail; when they have made audible to the historian that Voice of the

* This would not be the first time, that these fascinating volumes had been recommended as a substitute for History—a ground of recommendation, to which I could not conscientiously accede, though some half dozen of these Novels with a perfect recollection of the contents of every page, I read over more often in the course of a year, than I can honestly put down to my own credit.

83

People which is the Voice of God—this Principle, I say, (or the Power, that is the subject of it) which by its very essence existing and working as an *Idea* only, except in the rare and predestined epochs of Growth and Reparation, might seem to many fitter matter for verse than for sober argument, I will, by way of compromise, and for the amusement of the reader, sum up in the rhyming prose of an old Puritan Poet, consigned to contempt by Mr. Pope,[7] but whose writings, with all their barren flats and dribbling common-place, contain nobler principles, profounder truths, and more that is properly and peculiarly *poetic* than are to be found in his * own works. The passage in question, however, I found occupying the last page on a flying-sheet of four leaves, entitled *England's Misery and Remedy, in a judicious Letter from an Utter-Barrister to his Special Friend, concerning Lieut.-Col. Lilburne's Imprisonment in Newgate, Sept.* 1645;[8] and I beg leave to borrow the introduction, together with the extract, or that part at least, which suited my purpose.

"Christian Reader, having a vacant place for some few Lines I have made bold to use some of Major George Withers, his verses out of Vox Pacifica, *page* 199.[9]

> "Let not your King and Parliament in *One*,
> Much less apart, mistake themselves for that
> Which is most worthy to be thought upon:
> Nor think they are, essentially, the State.

---

* If it were asked whether the Author then considers the works of the one of equal value with those of the other, or that he holds George Withers as great a writer as Alexander Pope? his answers would be, that he is as little likely to do so, as the Querist would be to put no greater value on a highly wrought vase of pure silver from the hand of a master, than on an equal weight of Copper Ore that contained a small per centage of separable Gold scattered through it. The Reader will be pleased to observe, that in the stanza here cited, the "State" is used in the largest sense, and as synonimous with the Realm, or entire Body Politic, including Church and *State*, in the narrower and special sense of the latter term. S. T. C.

Let them not fancy, that th' Authority
And Priviledges upon them bestown,
Conferr'd are to set up a MAJESTY,
A POWER, or a GLORY of their own!
But let them know, 'twas for a deeper life,
Which they but *represent*——
That there's on earth a yet auguster Thing,
Veil'd tho' it be, than Parliament and King."

1. 'or, that ... any', added in second edition.
2. *The Royalist's Defence, Vindicating the King's Proceedings in the late War made against him.*
3. 'Whatever the King with Parliament has willed, let it be for an oracle'; with a play on 'factum sit', 'let it be done'.
4. In the first edition is inserted after 'idea', '(i.e., the interests of the proprietage of the realm, and (though not directly or formally, yet actually) the interests of the realm in its foreign relations, as affecting the weal, and requiring the aid of the proprietors)'.
5. An Act of 1716 providing that 'all Parliaments shall and may respectively have continuance for seven years, and no longer'. It was intended partly to allow the Hanoverian dynasty time to establish itself, and was zealously opposed by the Jacobites.
6. Convocation was prorogued by Royal Writ in 1717, after a dispute between the high-churchmen of the Lower House and the Whig Bishops of the Upper House, concerning a sermon preached by Hoadley, Bishop of Bangor; thereafter Convocation met only formally.
7. See the *Dunciad*, I. 296.
8. John Lilburne (1615–57), a leader of the Levellers.
9. George Wither (1588–1667), poet, pamphleteer, and major in the parliament army; *Vox Pacifica* was published in 1645; some sixteen lines of the original (*VP*, p. 169) omitted in *England's Misery*, and the last lines considerably altered by Coleridge.

CHAPTER XII

The preceding position exemplified. The origin and rationale of the Coronation Oath, in respect of the National Church. In what its moral obligation consists. Recapitulation.

AND here again the "Royalist's Defence" furnishes me with the introductory paragraph: and I am always glad to find in the words of an elder writer, what I must otherwise have said in my own person—*otium simul et autoritatem.*[1]

"All Englishmen grant, that Arbitrary power is destructive of the best purposes for which power is conferred: and in the preceding chapter it has been shown, that to give an unlimited authority over the fundamental Laws and Rights of the nation, even to the King and two Houses of Parliament jointly, though nothing so bad as to have this boundless power in the King alone, or in the Parliament alone, were nevertheless to deprive Englishmen of the Security from Arbitrary Power, which is their birth right.

"Upon perusal of former statutes it appears, that the Members of both Houses have been *frequently* drawn to consent, not only to things *prejudicial* to the Commonwealth, but, (even in matters of greatest weight) to alter and contradict what formerly themselves had agreed to, and that, as it happened to please the fancy of the present Prince, or to suit the passions and interests of a prevailing Faction. Witness the statute by which it was enacted that the Proclamation of King Henry VIII. should be equivalent to an Act of Parliament;[2] another declaring both Mary and Elizabeth bastards; and a third statute empowering the King to dispose of the Crown of England by Will and

Testament.[3] Add to these the several statutes in the times of King Henry VIII., Edward VI., Queen Mary, and Queen Elizabeth, setting up and pulling down each other's religion, every one of them condemning even to death the profession of the one before established."—*Royalist's Defence*, p. 41.

So far my anonymous author, evidently an old Tory Lawyer of the genuine breed, too enlightened to obfuscate and incense-blacken the shrine, through which the kingly Idea should be translucent, into an Idol to be worshipped in its own right; but who, considering both the reigning Sovereign and the Houses, as limited and representative functionaries, thought they saw reason, in some few cases, to place more confidence in the former than in the latter: while there were points, which they wished as little as possible to trust to either. With this experience, however, as above stated, (and it would not be difficult to increase the catalogue,) can we wonder that the nation grew sick of parliamentary *Religions*? or that the Idea should at last awake and become operative, that what virtually concerned their humanity, and involved yet higher relations, than those of the citizen to the state, duties more awful, and more precious privileges, while yet it stood in closest connection with all their *civil* duties and rights, as their indispensable condition and only secure ground—that this was not a matter to be voted up or down, off or on, by fluctuating majorities! that it was too precious an inheritance to be left at the discretion of an Omnipotency, that had so little claim to Omniscience? No interest of a single generation, but an entailed Boon too sacred, too momentous, to be shaped and twisted, pared down or plumped up, by any assemblage of Lords, Knights, and Burgesses for the time being? Men perfectly competent, it may be, to the protection and management of those interests, in which, as having so large a stake they may be reasonably presumed to feel a sincere and lively concern, but who, the experience of ages might teach us, are not the class of persons most likely to study, or feel a deep concern in, the interests here spoken of, in either sense of the term CHURCH; *i.e.* whether the interests be of a kingdom "not of the World," or those of an

Estate of the Realm, and a constituent part, therefore, of the same System with the State, though as the opposite Pole. The results at all events have been such, whenever the Representatives of the One Interest have assumed the direct control of the other, as gave occasion long ago to the rhyming couplet, quoted as proverbial by Luther:

> Cum Mare siccatur, cum Dæmon ad astra levatur,
> Tunc Clero Laicus fidus Amicus erit.[4]

But if the nation willed to withdraw the religion of the realm from the changes and revolutions incident to whatever is subjected to the suffrages of the representative assemblies, whether of the state or of the church, the trustees of the proprietage or those of the nationalty, the first question is, how this reservation is to be declared, and by what means to be effected. These means, the security for the permanence of the established religion, must, it may be foreseen, be imperfect; for what can be otherwise, that depends on human will? but yet it may be abundantly sufficient to declare the aim and intention of the provision. Our ancestors did the best it was in their power to do. Knowing by recent experience that multitudes never blush, that numerous assemblies, however respectably composed, are not exempt from temporary hallucinations, and the influence of party passion; that there are things, for the conservation of which—

> Men safelier trust to heaven, than to themselves,
> When least themselves, in storms of loud debate
> Where folly is contagious, and too oft
> Even wise men leave their better sense at home
> To chide and wonder at them, when returned.
>
> ZAPOLYA.[5]

Knowing this, our ancestors chose to place their reliance on the honour and conscience of an individual, whose comparative height, it was believed, would exempt him from the gusts and shifting currents, that agitate the lower region of the political atmosphere. Accordingly, on a change of dynasty they bound the person, who had accepted the crown in trust—

bound him for himself and his successors by an oath, to refuse his consent (without which no change in the existing law can be effected), to any measure subverting or tending to subvert the safety and independence of the National Church, or which exposed the realm to the danger of a return of that foreign usurper, misnamed spiritual, from which it had with so many sacrifices emancipated itself.[6] However unconstitutional therefore the royal veto on a Bill presented by the Lords and Commons may be deemed in all ordinary cases, this is clearly an exception. For it is no additional power conferred on the king; but a limit imposed on him by the constitution itself for its own safety. Previously to the ceremonial act, which announces him the only lawful and sovereign head of both the church and the state, the oath is administered to him *religiously* as the representative person and crowned majesty of the nation. *Religiously*, I say, for the mind of the nation, existing only as an *Idea*, can act *distinguishably* on the ideal powers alone—that is, on the reason and conscience.

It only remains then to determine, what it is to which the Coronation Oath obliges the conscience of the king. And this may be best determined by considering what in reason and in conscience the Nation had a right to impose. Now that the Nation had a right to decide for the King's conscience and reason, and for the reason and conscience of all his successors, and of his and their counsellors and ministers, laic and ecclesiastic, on questions of theology, and controversies of faith—*ex. gr.* that it is not allowable in directing our thoughts to a departed Saint, the Virgin Mary for instance, to say Or*a* pro nobis, Beata Virgo, though there would be no harm in saying, Or*et* pro nobis, precor, beata Virgo;[7] whether certain books are to be held canonical; whether the text, "They shall be saved as through fire,"[8] refers to a purgatorial process in the body, or during the interval between its dissolution and the day of judgment; whether the words, "this is my body," are to be understood literally, and if so, whether it is by consubstantiation with, or transubstantiation of, bread and wine; and that the members of both Houses of Parliament, together with the Privy Counsellors and all the Clergy shall abjure and denounce the theory last mentioned—this I utterly deny. And if this were the whole and sole object and intention of the Oath, however large the number might be of the persons who imposed or were notoriously favorable to the imposition, so far from recognizing the Nation in their collective number, I should regard them as no other than an aggregate of intolerant mortals, from bigotry and presumption forgetful of their fallibility, and not less ignorant of their own rights, than callous to those of succeeding generations. If the articles of faith therein disclaimed and denounced were the substance and proper intention of the Oath, and not to be understood, as in all common sense they ought to be, as temporary marks because the known accompaniments of other and legitimate grounds of disqualification; and which only in reference to *these*, and only as long as they implied their existence, were fit objects of political interference; it would be as impossible for me, as for the late Mr. Canning, to attach any such sanctity to the Coronation Oath,[9] as should prevent it from being superannuated in times of clearer light and less heat. But that these theological articles, and the open profession of the same by a portion of the king's subjects [10] as parts of their creed, are not the evils which it is the true and legitimate purpose of the oath to preclude, and which constitute and define its obligation on the royal conscience; and what the real evils are, that do indeed disqualify for offices of national trust, and give the permanent obligatory character to the engagement—this, in which I include the exposition of the essential characters of the Christian or Catholic Church; and of a very different church, which assumes the name; and the application of the premises to an appreciation on principle of the late bill, and now the law of the land; will occupy the remaining portion of the volume.

And now I may be permitted to look back on the road, we have past: in the course of which, I have placed before you, patient fellow-traveller! a small part indeed of what might, on a suitable occasion, be profitably said; but it is all, that for my present purpose, I deem it necessary to say respecting three out of the five themes that were to form the subjects of the first part of this—small volume, shall I call it? or large and dilated epistle? But let me avail myself of the pause, to repeat my apology to the reader for any *extra* trouble I may have imposed on him, by employing the same term (the State, namely) in two senses; though I flatter myself, I have in each instance so guarded it as to leave scarcely the possibility, that a moderately attentive reader should understand the word in one sense, when I had meant it in the other, or confound the STATE as a *whole*, and comprehending the Church, with the State as one of the two constituent parts, and in contra-distinction from the Church.

BRIEF RECAPITULATION.

First then, I have given briefly but, I trust, with sufficient clearness the right idea of a STATE, or Body Politic; 'State' being here synonimous with a *constituted* Realm, Kingdom, Commonwealth, or Nation, *i.e.* where the integral parts, classes, or orders are so balanced, or interdependent, as to constitute, more or less, a moral unit, an organic whole; and as arising out of the Idea of a State I have added the Idea of a Constitution, as the informing principle of its coherence and unity. But in applying the above to our own kingdom (and with this qualification the reader is requested to understand me as speaking in all the following remarks), it was necessary to observe, and I willingly avail myself of this opportunity to repeat the observation—that the Constitution, in its widest sense as the Constitution of the Realm, arose out of, and in fact consisted in, the co-existence of the Constitutional STATE (in the second acceptation of the term) with the King as its head, and of the CHURCH (*i.e.* the *National* Church), likewise the King as its head; and lastly of the King, as the Head and Majesty of the whole Nation. The reader was cautioned therefore not to confound it with either of its constituent parts; that he must first master the true idea of each of these severally; and that in the synopsis or conjunction of the three, the Idea of the English Constitution, the Constitution of the Realm, will rise of itself before him. And in aid of this purpose and following this order, I have given according to my best judgment, first, the Idea of the State, (in the second or *special* sense of the term;) of the State-legislature; and of the two constituent orders, the landed, with its two classes, the Major Barons, and the Franklins; and the Personal, consisting of the mercantile, or commercial, the manufacturing, the distributive and the professional; these two orders corresponding to the two great all-including INTERESTS of the State,—the landed, namely, to the PERMANENCE,—the Personal to the PROGRESSION. The Possessions of both orders, taken collectively, form the * PRO-PRIETAGE of the Realm. In contradistinction from this and as my second theme, I have explained (and as being the principal object of this work, more diffusely) the NATIONALTY, its nature and purposes, and the duties and qualifications of its Trustees and Functionaries. In the same sense as I at once oppose and conjoin the NATIONALTY to the PROPRIETAGE; in the same antithesis and conjunction I use and understand the phrase, CHURCH and STATE. Lastly, I have essayed to determine the Constitutional Idea of the CROWN, and its relations to the Nation, to which I have added a few sentences on the relations of the Nation to the State.

To the completion of this first part of my undertaking, two subjects still remain to be treated of—and to each of these I shall devote a small section, the title of the first being "On the Idea of the Christian Church;" that of the other, "On a third Church:" the name of which I withhold for the present, in the expectation of deducing it by contrast from the contra-distinguishing characters of the former.

* To convey his meaning precisely is a *debt*, which an Author owes to his readers. He therefore who to escape the charge of pedantry, will rather be misunderstood than startle a fastidious critic with an unusual term, may be compared to the man who should pay his creditor, in base or counterfeit coin, when he had gold or silver ingots in his possession, to the precise amount of the debt; and this under the pretence of their unshapeliness and want of the mint impression.

1. 'At once a source of leisure [in that the work has already been done for Coleridge by an earlier writer] and an authority [to cite].'
2. An Act of 1539, repealed in the first year of Edward VI.
3. The Succession Acts of 1536 and 1544.
4. 'When the sea runs dry, and the Devil is raised to the stars, then will the Layman be a faithful friend to the Cleric'; *Colloquia Mensalia*, tr. Bell (London 1652), ch. 22.
5. Coleridge, *Zapolya*, I. i. 368–72, slightly altered.
6. This provision was first included in the Coronation Oath by an act of 1689 (1 Wm. & M. c. 6), by which the king at his coronation was obliged to swear that he would maintain 'the Protestant Reformed Religion Established by Law'. This part of the oath became an important obstacle to Catholic Relief in the reigns of George III and George IV, who felt bound by it to prevent the repeal of the Test Acts.
7. 'Pray for us, blessed Virgin'; 'I beg that the blessed Virgin may pray for us.' Coleridge refers to articles of belief included in the declaration which was a part of the second Test Act (1678), repeated by the monarch at his coronation.
8. 1 Corinthians iii. 15; the text from which the doctrine of purgatory is derived.
9. See Canning, *Speeches*: 'On the Catholic Claims', vol. III. 320–1; 'On the Catholic Question', vol. VI. 165.
10. 'the open . . . subjects'; 'the exclusion of all who professed to receive them', 1st edition.

IDEA

OF

THE CHRISTIAN CHURCH.

'WE, (said Luther), tell our Lord God plainly: If he will have his Church, then He must look how to maintain and defend it; for we can neither uphold nor protect it. And well for us, that it is so! For in case we could, or were able to defend it, we should become the proudest Asses under heaven. Who is the Church's Protector, that hath promised to be with her to the end, and the gates of Hell shall not prevail against her? Kings, Diets, Parliaments, Lawyers? Marry, no such cattle.'—*Colloquia Mensalia.*[1]

IDEA OF THE CHRISTIAN CHURCH.

THE practical conclusion from our enquiries respecting the origin and Idea of the National Church, the paramount end and purpose of which is the continued and progressive civilization of the community (*emollit mores nec sinit esse feros*),[2] was this: that though many things may be conceived of a tendency to diminish the *fitness* of particular men, or of a particular class, to be chosen as trustees and functionaries of the same; though there may be many points more or less adverse to the perfection of the establishment; there are yet but two absolute disqualifications: namely, allegiance to a foreign power, or an acknowledgment of any other visible head of the Church, but our sovereign lord the king; and compulsory celibacy in connection with, and dependence on, a foreign and extra-national head. We are now called to a different contemplation, to the Idea of the Christian Church.

OF the Christian *Church*, I say, not of Christianity. To the ascertainment and enucleation of the latter, of the great redemptive process which began in the separation of light from Chaos (*Hades, or the Indistinction*), and has its end in the union of life with God, the whole summer and autumn, and now commenced winter of my life have been dedicated. HIC labor, HOC opus est,[3]

97

on which alone the author rests his hope, that he shall be found not to have lived altogether in vain. Of the Christian *Church* only, and of this no further than is necessary for the distinct understanding of the National Church, it is my purpose now to speak: and for this purpose it will be sufficient to enumerate the essential characters by which the Christian church is distinguished.

FIRST CHARACTER.—The Christian Church is not a KINGDOM, REALM, (*royaume*), or STATE, (*sensu latiori*) [4] of the WORLD, that is, of the aggregate, or total number of the kingdoms, states, realm, or bodies politic, (these words being as far as our present argument is concerned, perfectly synonimous), into which civilized man is distributed; and which, collectively taken, constitute the civilized WORLD. The Christian Church, I say, is no state, kingdom, or realm of this world; nor is it an Estate of any such realm, kingdom or state; but it is the appointed Opposite to them all *collectively*—the *sustaining, correcting, befriending* Opposite of the world! the compensating counterforce to the inherent * and inevitable evils and defects

---

* It is not without pain that I have advanced this position, without the accompanying proofs and documents which it may be thought to require, and without the elucidations which I am sure it deserves; but which are precluded alike by the purpose and the limits of the present tract. I will, however, take this opportunity of earnestly recommending to such of my readers as understand German, Lessing's ERNST und FALK: Gespräche für Freymäurer. They will find it in Vol. vii. of the Leipsic edition of Lessing's Works. I am not aware of a translation.[5] Mr. Blackwood, or I should say Christopher North,[6] would add one to the very many obligations he has already conferred on his readers, (among whom he has few more constant or more thankful than myself) by suggesting the task to some of his contributors. For there are more than one, I doubt not, who possess taste to feel, and power to transfer the point, elegance, and exquisite, yet effortless precision and conciseness of Lessing's philosophic and controversial writings. I know nothing that is at once like them, and equal to them, but the Provincial Letters of Pascal. The four Dialogues, to which I have referred, would not occupy much more than a quarter of a sheet each, in his magazine,

of the STATE, *as* a State, and without reference to its better or worse construction as a particular state; while whatever is beneficent and humanizing in the aims, tendencies, and proper objects of the state, the Christian Church collects in itself as in a focus, to radiate them back in a higher quality: or to change the metaphor, it completes and strengthens the edifice of the state, without interference or commixture, in the mere act of laying and securing its own foundations. And for these services the Church of Christ asks of the state neither wages nor dignities. She asks only protection, and *to be let alone*. These indeed she demands; but even these only on the ground, that there is nothing in her constitution, nor in her discipline, inconsistent with the interests of the state, nothing resistant or impedimental to the state in the exercise of its rightful powers, in the fulfilment of its appropriate duties, or in the effectuation of its legitimate objects. It is a fundamental principle of all legislation, that the state shall leave the largest portion of personal free agency to each of its citizens, that is compatible with the free agency of all, and not subversive of the ends of its own existence as a state. And though a negative, it is a most important distinctive character of the Church of Christ, that she asks nothing for her members as Christians, which they are not already entitled to demand as citizens and subjects.

SECOND CHARACTER.—The Christian Church is not a secret community. In the once current (and well worthy to be reissued) terminology of our elder divines, it is objective in its nature and purpose, not mystic or subjective, *i.e.* not like reason or the court of conscience, existing only in and for the individual. Consequently the church here spoken of is not "the

---

which, in a deliberate and conscientious adoption of a very commonplace compliment, I profess to think, as a magazine, and considering the number of years it has *kept on the wing—incomparable*—but at the same time I crave the venerable Christopher's permission to avow myself a sturdy dissentient as on some other points, so especially from the *Anti-Huskissonian* part of his Toryism.[7]   S. T. C.

kingdom of God which is *within*, and which cometh not with observation (*Luke* xvii. 20, 21), but most observable (*Luke* xxi. 28–31)."—A city built on a hill, and not to be hid [8]—an institution consisting of visible and public communities. In one sentence, it is the Church visible and militant under Christ. And this visibility, this *publicity*, is its second distinctive character. The

THIRD CHARACTER—reconciles the two preceding, and gives the condition, under which their co-existence in the same subject becomes possible. Antagonist forces are necessarily of the same kind. It is an old rule of logic, that only concerning two subjects of the same kind can it be properly said that they are opposites. Inter res heterogeneas non datur oppositio, *i.e.* contraries cannot be opposites. Alike in the primary and the metaphorical use of the word, Rivals (Rivales) are those only who inhabit the opposite banks of *the same stream.*

Now, in conformity to character the first, the Christian Church dare not be considered as a counter-pole to any particular STATE, the word, State, here taken in the largest sense. Still less can it, like the national clerisy, be opposed to the STATE in the narrower sense. The *Christian* Church, as such, has no *nationalty* entrusted to its charge. It forms no counterbalance to the collective *heritage* of the realm. The phrase, Church and State, has a sense and a propriety in reference to the *National* Church alone. The Church of Christ cannot be placed in this conjunction and antithesis without forfeiting the very name of Christian. The true and only contra-position of the Christian Church is to the world. Her paramount aim and object, indeed, is *another* world, not a world *to come* exclusively, but likewise *another world that now is* (*See* APPENDIX, A),[9] and to the concerns of which alone the epithet spiritual, can without a mischievous abuse of the word, be applied. But as the necessary consequence and accompaniments of the means by which she seeks to attain this especial end; and as a collateral object, it is her office to counteract the evils that result by a common necessity from all Bodies Politic, the system or aggregate of which is the WORLD. And observe that the nisus, or counteragency, of the Christian Church is against the evil *results* only, and not (directly, at least, or by primary intention) against the defective institutions that may have caused or aggravated them.

But on the other hand, by virtue of the second character, the Christian Church is to exist in every kingdom and state of the world, in the form of public communities, is to exist as a real and ostensible power. The consistency of the first and second depends on, and is fully effected by, the

THIRD CHARACTER

of the Church of Christ: namely, the absence of any visible head or sovereign—by the non-existence, nay the utter preclusion, of any local or personal centre of unity, of any single source of universal power. This fact may be thus illustrated. Kepler [10] and Newton, substituting the idea of the infinite for the conception of a finite and determined world, assumed in the Ptolemaic Astronomy, superseded and drove out the notion of a one central point or body of the Universe. Finding a centre in every point of matter and an absolute circumference no where, they explained at once the unity and the distinction that co-exist throughout the creation by focal instead of central bodies: the attractive and restraining power of the sun or focal orb, in each particular system, supposing and resulting from an actual power, present in all and over all, throughout an indeterminable multitude of systems. And this, demonstrated as it has been by science, and verified by observation, we rightly name the true system of the heavens. And even such is the scheme and true idea of the Christian Church. In the primitive times, and as long as the churches retained the form given them by the Apostles and Apostolic men, every community, or in the words of a father of the second century,[11] (for the pernicious fashion of assimilating the Christian to the Jewish, as afterwards to the Pagan, Ritual, by false analogies, was almost coeval with the church itself,) every altar had its own bishop, every flock its own pastor, who derived his authority immediately from Christ, the universal Shepherd, and acknowledged no other superior than the same Christ, speaking by his spirit in the unanimous decision of any number of bishops or elders, according to his promise, "*Where two or three are gathered together in my name, there am I in the midst of them.*" [12] *

* Questions of dogmatic divinity do not enter into the purpose of this enquiry. I am even anxious not to give the work a theological character. It is, however, within the scope of my argument to observe, that, as may be incontrovertibly proved by other equivalent declarations of our Lord, this promise is not confined to houses of worship and prayer-meetings exclusively. And though I cannot offer the same justification for what follows, yet the interest and importance of the subject will, I trust, excuse me if I remark, that even in reference to meetings for divine worship, the true import of these gracious, soul-awing words, is too generally overlooked. It is not the comments or harangues of unlearned and fanatical preachers that I have in my mind, but sermons of great and deserved celebrity, and divines whose learning, well-regulated zeal, and sound scriptural views are as honourable to the established church, as their piety, beneficence, and blameless life, are to the Christian name, when I say that passages occur which might almost lead one to conjecture, that the authors had found the words, "*I will come and join you,*" instead of, "I am in the midst of you,"—(Compare I. *John*, iii. 24)—passages from which it is at least difficult not to infer, that they had interpreted the promise, as of a corporal co-presence, instead of a spiritual *immanence* ($ὅτι\ μένει\ ἐν\ ἡμῖν$) [13] as of an individual coming in or down, and taking *a place*, as soon as the required number of petitioners was completed! As if, in short, this presence, this actuation of the "I AM," ($εἰμὶ\ ἐν\ μέσῳ\ αὐτῶν$) [14] were an after-consequence, an accidental and separate result and reward of the contemporaneous and contiguous worshipping—and not the total act itself, of which the spiritual Christ, one and the same in all the faithful, is the originating and perfective focal unity. Even as the physical life *is* in each limb and organ of the body, "all in every part"; but is *manifested* as life, by being one in all and thus making all *one*: even so with Christ, our Spiritual Life! He *is* in each true believer, in his solitary prayer and during his silent communion in the watches of the night, no less than in the congregation of the faithful; but he *manifests* his indwelling presence more characteristically, with

Hence the unitive relation of the churches to each other, and of each to all, being equally *actual* indeed, but likewise equally IDEAL, *i.e.* mystic and supersensual, as the relation of the

---

especial evidence, when many, convened in his name, whether for prayer or for council, do through him become ONE.

I would that these preceding observations were as little connected with the main subject of this volume, as to some they will appear to be! But as the mistaking of symbols and analogies for metaphors (See *Aids to Reflection*, pp. 198, 254, G. 398,) has been a main occasion and support of the worst errors in Protestantism; so the understanding the same symbols in a literal *i.e. phænomenal* sense, notwithstanding the most earnest warnings against it, the most express declarations of the folly and danger of interpreting *sensually* what was delivered of objects *super*-sensual—this was the rank wilding, on which "the prince of this world," the lust of power and worldly aggrandizement, was enabled to graft, one by one, the whole branchery of papal superstition and imposture. A truth not less important might be conveyed by reversing the image—by representing the papal monarchy as the stem or trunk circulating a poison-sap through the branches successively grafted thereon, the previous and natural fruit of which was at worst only mawkish and innutritious. Yet among the dogmas or articles of belief that contradistinguish the Roman Catholic from the Reformed Churches, the most important and, in their practical effects and consequences, the most pernicious, I cannot but regard as refracted and distorted truths, profound ideas sensualized into idols, or at the lowest rate lofty and affecting imaginations, safe while they remained general and indefinite, but debased and rendered noxious by their application in detail: *ex. gr.* the doctrine of the Communion of Saints, or the sympathy between all the members of the universal church, which death itself doth not interrupt, exemplified in St. Anthony and the cure of sore eyes, St. Boniface and success in brewing, &c. &c. &c. What the same doctrines now are, used as the pretexts and shaped into the means and implements of priestly power and revenue: or rather, what the whole scheme *is* of Romish rites, doctrines, institutions, and practices in their combined and full operation, where it exists in undisputed sovereignty, neither repressed by the prevalence, nor modified by the light of a purer faith, nor held in check by the consciousness of Protestant neighbours and lookers-on—this is

whole church to its one invisible Head, the church with and under Christ, as a one kingdom or state, is hidden: while from all its several component monads, (the particular visible

---

a question, which cannot be kept too distinct from the former. And, as at the risk of passing for a secret favourer of superannuated superstitions, I have spoken out my thoughts of the Catholic theology, so, and at a far more serious risk of being denounced as an intolerant bigot, I will declare what, after a two years' residence in exclusively Catholic countries, and in situations and under circumstances that afforded more than ordinary means of acquainting myself with the workings and the proceeds of the machinery, was the impression left on my mind as to the effects and influences of the Romish (most *un*-Catholic) religion,—not as even according to its own canons and authorised decisions it *ought* to be; but, as it actually and practically exists.—(*See this distinction ably and eloquently enforced in a Catholic work, intitled* RIFORMA D'ITALIA).[15] This impression, and the convictions grounded thereon, which have assuredly not been weakened by the perusal of the Rev. Blanco White's [16] most affecting statements, and by the recent history of Spain and Portugal,[17] I cannot convey more satisfactorily to myself than by repeating the answer, which I long since returned to the same question put by a friend, viz.—

When I contemplate the whole system, as it affects the great fundamental principles of morality, the *terra firma*, as it were, of our humanity; then trace its operation on the sources and conditions of national strength and well-being; and lastly, consider its woeful influences on the innocence and sanctity of the female mind and imagination, on the faith and happiness, the gentle fragrancy and unnoticed ever-present verdure of domestic life—I can with difficulty avoid applying to it what the Rabbins fable of the fratricide CAIN, after the curse: that *the firm earth trembled wherever he strode, and the grass turned black beneath his feet.*[18]

Indeed, if my memory does not cheat me, some of the "mystic divines," in their fond humour of allegorizing, tell us, that in Gen. iv. 3—8, is correctly narrated the history of the first apostate church, that began by sacrificing amiss, impropriating the fruit of *the ground* (*i.e.* temporal possessions) under spiritual pretexts; and ended in slaying the shepherd brother who brought " the firstlings of his fold," [19] holy and without blemish, to the Great Shepherd, and presented them as "*new* creatures," before the Lord and Owner of the Flocks.—S. T. C.

churches I mean,) Cæsar receiving the things that are Cæsar's, and confronted by no rival Cæsar, by no authority, which existing locally, temporally, and in the person of a fellow mortal, must be essentially of the same *kind* with his own, notwithstanding any attempt to belie its true nature under the perverted and contradictory name of *spiritual*, sees only so many loyal groups, who, claiming no peculiar rights, make themselves known to him as Christians, only by the more scrupulous and exemplary performance of their duties as citizens and subjects. And here let me add a few sentences on the use, abuse, and misuse of the phrase, *spiritual* Power. In the only appropriate sense of the words, *spiritual* power is a power that acts on the *spirits* of men. Now the spirit of a man, or the spiritual part of our being, is the intelligent Will: or (to speak less abstractly) it is the capability, with which the Father of Spirits hath endowed man of being determined to action by the *ultimate ends*, which the reason alone can present. (The Understanding, which derives all its materials from the Senses, can dictate *purposes* only, *i.e.* such ends as are in their turn *means* to other ends.) The ultimate ends, by which the will is to be determined, and by which alone the will, not corrupted, "*the spirit made perfect*," [20] *would* be determined, are called, in relation to the Reason, moral *Ideas*. Such are the Ideas of the Eternal, the Good, the True, the Holy, the Idea of God as the Absoluteness and Reality (or real ground) of all these, or as the Supreme Spirit in which all these substantially *are*, and are ONE. Lastly, the idea of the responsible will itself; of duty, of guilt, or evil in itself without reference to its outward and separable consequences, &c. &c.

A power, therefore, that acts on the appetites and passions, which we possess in common with the beasts, by motives derived from the senses and sensations, has no pretence to the name; nor can it without the grossest abuse of the word be called a *spiritual* power. Whether the man expects the *auto de fé*, the fire and faggots, with which he is threatened, to take place at Lisbon or Smithfield, or in some dungeon in the centre of the earth, makes no difference in the *kind* of motive by which he is influenced; nor of course in the nature of the power, which acts on his passions by means of it. It would be strange indeed, if ignorance and superstition, the dense and rank fogs that most strangle and suffocate the light of the spirit in man, should constitute a spirituality in the power, which takes advantage of them!

This is a gross *abuse* of the term, spiritual. The following, sanctioned as it is by custom and statute, yet (speaking exclusively as a philologist and without questioning its legality) I venture to point out, as a *misuse* of the term. Our great Church dignitaries sit in the Upper House of the Convocation, as *Prelates* of the National Church: and as *Prelates*, may exercise *ecclesiastical* power. In the House of Lords they sit as *barons*, and by virtue of the baronies which, much against the will of those haughty prelates, our kings forced upon them: and as such, they exercise a *Parliamentary* power. As bishops of the Church of Christ only can they possess, or exercise (and God forbid! I should doubt, that as such, many of them do faithfully exercise) a *spiritual* power, which neither king can give, nor King and Parliament take away. As Christian *bishops*, they are spiritual *pastors*, by power of the spirit ruling the flocks committed to their charge; but they are *temporal* peers and prelates. The

FOURTH CHARACTER

of the Christian Church, and a necessary consequence of the first and third, is its Catholicity, *i.e.* universality. It is neither Anglican, Gallican, nor Roman, neither Latin nor Greek. Even the Catholic and Apostolic Church *of* England is a less safe expression than the Churches of Christ in England: though the Catholic Church *in* England, or (what would be still better,) the Catholic Church under Christ throughout Great Britain and Ireland, is justifiable and appropriate: for through the presence of its only head and sovereign, entire in each and one in all, the Church universal is spiritually perfect in every true Church, and of course in any number of such Churches, which from circumstance of place, or the community of country or of language, we have occasion to speak of collectively. (I have already, here and elsewhere, observed, and scarcely a day passes without some occasion to repeat the observation, that an equivocal term, or a word with two or more different meanings, is never quite harmless. Thus, it is at least an inconvenience in our language, that the term Church, instead of being confined to its proper sense, Kirk, Ædes Kyriacæ, or the Lord's House, should likewise be the word by which our forefathers rendered the ecclesia, or the eccleti (ἐκκλήτοι) i.e. evocati, the called out of the world, named collectively; and likewise our term for the clerical establishment. To the Called at Rome—to the Church of Christ at Corinth—or in Philippi—such was the language of the apostolic age; and the change since then has been no improvement.) The true Church *of* England is the National Church, or Clerisy. There exists, God be thanked! a Catholic and Apostolic church *in* England: and I thank God also for the Constitutional and Ancestral Church *of* England.

These are the four distinctions, or peculiar and essential marks, by which the church with Christ as its head is distinguished from the National Church, and *separated* from every possible counterfeit, that has, or shall have, usurped its name. And as an important comment on the same, and in confirmation of the principle which I have attempted to establish, I earnestly recommend for the reader's perusal, the following transcript from DR. HENRY MORE's *Modest Enquiry, or True Idea of Antichristianism.*[21]

"We will suppose some one prelate, who had got the start of the rest, to put in for the title and authority of Universal Bishop: and for the obtaining of this sovereignty, he will first pretend, that it is unfit that the visible Catholic Church, being one, should not be united under one visible head, which reasoning, though it makes a pretty shew at first sight, will yet, being closely looked into, vanish into smoke. For this is but a quaint concinnity urged in behalf of an impossibility. For the erecting such an office for one man, which no one *man* in the world is able to perform, implies that to be possible which is indeed impossible. Whence it is plain that the *head* will be *too little for the body*; which therefore will be a piece of mischievous assymmetry or inconcinnity also. No one mortal can be a competent head for that church which has a right to be *Catholic*, and to overspread the face of the whole earth. There can be no such head but Christ, who is not mere man, but God in the Divine humanity, and therefore present with every part of the church, and every member thereof, at what distance soever. But to set some one mortal bishop over the whole church, were to suppose that great bishop of our spirit absent from it, who has promised that he *will be with her to the end of the world*. Nor does the Church Catholic on earth lose her unity thereby. For rather hereby only is or can she be one. "As rationally might it be pretended, that it is not the Life, the *Rector Spiritus præsens per totum et in omni parte*,[22] but the Crown of the skull, or some one Convolute of the brain, that causes and preserves the unity of the Body Natural."—*Inserted by the transcriber*.

Such and so futile is the first pretence. But if this will not serve the turn, there is another in reserve. And notwithstanding the demonstrated impossibility of the thing, still there must be one visible head of the church universal, the successor and vicar of Christ, *for the slaking of controversies*, for the determination of disputed points! We will not stop here to expose the weakness of the argument (not alas! peculiar to the sophists of Rome, nor employed in support of *papal* infallibility only), that this or that *must be*, and consequently *is*, because sundry inconveniences would result from the want of it! and this without considering whether these inconveniences *have been* prevented or removed by its (pretended) presence; whether they do not continue in spite of this pretended remedy or antidote; whether these inconveniences were *intended* by providence to be precluded, and not rather for wise purposes permitted to continue; and lastly, whether the remedy may not be worse than the disease, like the sugar of lead administered by the Empiric, who cured a fever fit by exchanging it for the dead palsy.[23] Passing by this sophism, therefore, it is sufficient to reply, that all points necessary are so plain and so widely known, that it is impossible that a Christian, who seeks those aids which the true head of the church has promised shall never be sought in vain, should err therein from lack of knowing better. And those who, from defects of head or heart, are blind to this widely diffused light, and who neither seek nor wish those aids, are still less likely to be influenced by a minor and derivative authority. But for other things, whether ceremonies or conceits, whether matters of discipline or of opinion, their diversity does not at all break the unity of the outward and visible church, as long as they do not subvert the fundamental laws of Christ's kingdom, nor contradict the terms of admission into his church, nor contravene the essential characters, by which it subsists, and is distinguished as the Christian Catholic Church.

To these sentiments, borrowed from one of the most philosophical of our learned elder Divines, I have only to add an observation as suggested by them—that as many and fearful mischiefs have ensued from the confusion of the Christian with the National Church, so have many and grievous practical errors, and much unchristian intolerance, arisen from confounding the outward and visible church of Christ, with the spiritual and invisible church, known only to the Father of all Spirits. The perfection of the former is to afford every opportunity, and to present no obstacle, to a gradual advancement in the latter. The different degrees of progress, the imperfections, errors and accidents of false perspective, which lessen indeed with our advance—spiritual *advance*—but to a greater or lesser amount are inseparable from all progression; these, the interpolated half-truths of the twilight, through which every soul must pass from darkness to the spiritual sunrise, belong to the visible church as objects of Hope, Patience, and Charity alone.

1. *Table Talk*, tr. Bell (1652), p. 265. 'Who is . . . cattle' inserted by Coleridge.
2. See above, note 5, ch. IX.
3. 'This is the work, this is the task.' *Aeneid* VI. 129.
4. 'in the wider sense'.

5. Coleridge means the Berlin edition. A translation of *Ernst und Falk* appeared in *Lessing's Masonic Dialogues*, tr. Cohen (London, 1927).
6. John Wilson (1785–1854), Professor of Moral Philosophy at Edinburgh, and as 'Christopher North' a leading contributor to *Blackwood's Magazine*.
7. William Huskisson (1770–1830), President of the Board of Trade 1823–7, advocate of Free Trade and like Coleridge an opponent of the Corn Laws; he was attacked several times in *Blackwood's*—see vols. XIX. 474ff; XXII. 135ff; XXIV. 107ff.
8. Matthew v. 14.
9. Only one appendix in all editions; was Coleridge intending a second?
10. Johannes Kepler (1571–1630), the discoverer of the laws of planetary motion.
11. Probably Clement of Rome, *Epistle to the Corinthians*, 42; this text is sometimes assigned to the early years of the second century, but more usually to the last decades of the first.
12. Matthew xviii. 20.
13. 'that which abides among us'.
14. 'I am in the midst of you.' All editions have ἐῖμι ('I will come'), surely an error for εἰμί ('I am').
15. See above, note 7, ch. IX.
16. See above, note 6, ch. IX.
17. Coleridge refers to the establishment of absolutist regimes, by Ferdinand VII in Spain, and by John VI and Dom Miguel in Portugal, which followed the revolutions in those countries in the early 1820s. In 1820 Ferdinand revoked a decree of 1813 by which the Inquisition had been declared 'incompatible with the constitution'.
18. For ref., see Ginzberg, *The Legends of the Jews* (Philadelphia, 1909–38), vols. I. p. 111; V. p. 141; also Graves and Patai, *The Hebrew Myths* (London, 1963), pp. 92–3.
19. Genesis iv. 4.
20. Hebrews xii. 23.
21. Dr Henry More (1614–87), theologian, one of the Cambridge Platonists; the quotation that follows (condensed and slightly altered) is from *A Modest Enquiry* (1664), p. 140.
22. 'Guiding Spirit present throughout the whole and in every part.'

23. A sugar of lead, or *saccharum saturni*, was commonly prescribed for fevers in the seventeenth and at the end of the eighteenth centuries. 'Though it may cure the fever, it is apt to leave a worse disorder behind it,' wrote H. Boerhaave, with whose *New Method of Chemistry*, tr. Shaw and Chambers (London, 1727), Coleridge was familiar, and from whose comments on *saccharum saturni* (op. cit., p. 277) this anecdote may be adapted.

ON THE

THIRD POSSIBLE CHURCH,

OR THE

CHURCH OF ANTICHRIST.

Ecclesia Cattolica non, ma il Papismo denunciamo, perchè suggerito dal Interesse, perchè fortificato dalla menzogna, perchè radicato dal piu abbominevole despotismo, perchè contrario al diritto e ai titoli incommunicabili di Cristo, ed alla tranquillità d'ogni Chiesa e d'ogni Stato.—SPANZOTTI.[1]

THUS, on the depluming of THE POPE, every bird had his own feather: in the partage whereof, what he had gotten by *Sacrilege*, was restored to Christ; what by *Usurpation*, was given to the king, the (National) Church and the State; what by *Oppression*, was remitted to each particular Christian.

Fuller's Church History of Britain, Book v.[2]

ON THE CHURCH, NEITHER NATIONAL NOR UNIVERSAL.

If our forefathers were annoyed with the *cant* of over-boiling zeal, arising out of the belief, that the Pope is Antichrist, and likewise (*sexu mutato*) the Harlot of Babylon: we are more endangered by the *twaddle* of humid charity, which (some years ago at least) used to drizzle, a something between mist and small rain, from the higher region of our church atmosphere. It was sanctioned, I mean, both in the pulpit and the senate by sundry dignitaries, whose horror of Jacobinism during the then panic of Property led them to adopt the principles and language of Laud and his faction.[3] And once more the Church of Rome, in contrast with the Protestant Dissenters, became "a right dear, though erring Sister." [4] And the heaviest charge against the Romish Pontificate was, that the Italian politics and Nepotism of a series of Popes had converted so great a good into an intolerable grievance. We were reminded, that Grotius and Leibnitz had regarded a visible head of the Catholic church as most desirable: [5] that they, and with them more than one Primate of our own church, yearned for a conciliating settlement of the differences between the Romish and Protestant churches; and mainly in order that there might exist *really*, as well as *nominally*, a visible head of the church universal, a fixt centre of unity. Of course the tenet, that the Pope was in any sense the Antichrist predicted by Paul, was decried as fanatical and puritanical cant.

Now it is a duty of Christian charity to presume, that the men, who in the present day employ this language, are, or believe themselves to be, Christians: and that they do not privately think that St. Paul, in the two celebrated passages of his First and Second Epistles to the Church of Thessalonica, (I. iv. 13–18; II ii. 1–12), practised a *ruse de guerre*, and meant only by throwing the fulfilment beyond the life of the present generation, and by a terrific detail of the horrors and calamities that were to precede it, to damp the impatience, and silence the objections, excited by the expectation and the delay of our Lord's personal re-appearance. Again: as the persons, of whom we have been speaking, are well educated men, and men of sober minds, we may safely take for granted, that they do not understand by Antichrist any nondescript monster, or suppose it to be the proper name or designation of some one individual man or devil exclusively. The Christians of the second century, sharing in a delusion that prevailed over the whole Roman Empire, believed that Nero would come to life again, and be Antichrist: and I have been informed, that a learned clergyman of our own times, endowed with the gift of prophecy by assiduous study of Daniel, and the Apocalypse, asserts the same thing of Napoleon Bonaparte.

But, as before said, it would be calumnious to attribute such pitiable fanaticism to the parties here in question. And to *them* I venture to affirm, that if by Antichrist be meant—what alone can rationally be meant—a power in the Christian church, which in the name of Christ, and at once pretending and usurping his authority, is systematically subversive of the essential and distinguishing characters and purposes of the Christian church: that *then*, if the papacy, and the Romish Hierarchy as far as it is papal, be *not* Antichrist, the guilt of schism, in its most aggravated form, lies on the authors of the Reformation. For nothing less than this could have justified so tremendous a rent in the Catholic church, with all its foreseen most calamitous consequences. And so Luther himself thought;

and so thought Wickliffe before him.[6] Only in the conviction that Christianity itself was at stake; that the cause was that of Christ in conflict with Antichrist: could, or did even the lion-hearted Luther with unquailed spirit avow to himself: I bring not peace, but a sword into the world.[7]

It is my full conviction, a conviction formed after a long and patient study of the subject in detail; and if the author in support of this competence only added that he has read, and with care, the Summa Theologiæ [8] of Aquinas, and compared the system with the statements of Arnold and Bossuet,[9] the number of those who in the present much-reading, but not very hard-reading age, would feel themselves entitled to dispute his claim, will not, perhaps, be very formidable——

It is, I repeat, my full conviction, that the rites and doctrines, the *agenda et credenda*,[10] of the Catholics, could we separate them from the adulterating ingredients combined with, and the use made of them, by the sacerdotal Mamelukes of the Romish monarchy, for the support of the Papacy and papal hierarchy, would neither have brought about, nor have sufficed to justify, the convulsive separation under Leo X.[11] Nay, that if they were fairly, and in the light of a sound philosophy, compared with either of the two main divisions of Protestantism, as it now exists in this country, *i.e.* with the fashionable doctrines and interpretations of the Arminian and Grotian school on the one hand,[12] and with the tenets and language of the modern Calvinists on the other, an enlightened disciple of John and of Paul would be perplexed, which of the three to prefer as the least unlike the profound and sublime system, he had learnt from his great masters. And in this comparison I leave out of view the extreme sects of Protestantism, whether of the Frigid or of the Torrid Zone, Socinian or fanatic.

During the summer of last year, I made the tour of Holland, Flanders, and up the Rhine as far as Bergen, and among the few notes then taken, I find the following:—"Every fresh opportunity of examining the Roman Catholic religion on the spot, every new fact that presents itself to my notice, increases my conviction, that its immediate basis, and the true grounds of its continuance, are to be found in the wickedness, ignorance, and wretchedness of the many; and that the producing and continuing cause of this deplorable state is, that it is the interest of the Romish Priesthood, that so it should remain, as the surest, and in fact, only support of the Papal Sovereignty and influence against the civil powers, and the reforms wished for by the more enlightened governments, as well as by all the better informed and wealthier class of Catholics generally. And as parts of the same policy, and equally indispensable to the interests of the Triple Crown,[13] are the ignorance, grossness, excessive number and poverty of the lower Ecclesiastics themselves, including the religious orders. N.B.—When I say the Pope, I understand the papal hierarchy, which is, in truth, the *dilated Pope*: and in this sense only, and not of the individual Priest or Friar at Rome, can a wise man be supposed to use the word."— COLOGNE, *July* 2, 1828.

I feel it as no small comfort and confirmation, to know that the same view of the subject is taken, the same conviction entertained, by a large and increasing number in the Catholic communion itself, in Germany, France, Italy, and even in Spain; and that no inconsiderable portion of this number consists of men who are not only pious as Christians, but zealous as Catholics; and who would contemplate with as much horror a Reform *from* their Church, as they look with earnest aspirations and desires towards a Reform *in* the Church. Proof of this may be found in the learned work, intitled "Disordini moralie politici della Corte di Roma,"[14]—evidently the work of a zealous Catholic, and from the ecclesiastical erudition displayed in the volumes, probably a Catholic priest. Nay, from the angry aversion with which the foul heresies of those sons of perdition, Luther and Calvin, are mentioned, and his very faint and qualified censure of the persecution of the Albigenses and Waldenses,[15] I am obliged to infer, that the writer's attachment to his communion was zealous even to bigotry!

The disorders denounced by him are:—

1. The pretension of the Papacy to temporal power and sovereignty, directly or as the pretended consequence of

spiritual dominion; and as furnishing occasion to this, even the retention of the primacy *in honour* over all other bishops, after Rome had ceased to be the metropolis of Christendom,[16] is noticed as a subject of regret.

2. The boast of papal infallibility.

3. *The derivation of the Episcopal Power from the Papal, and the dependence of Bishops on the Pope, rightly named the evil of a false centre.*

4. The right of exercising authority in other dioceses besides that of Rome.

5. The privilege of reserving to himself the *greater causes—le cause maggiori.*[17]

6, 7, 8, 9, 10. Of conferring any and every benefice in the territory of other bishops; of exacting the Annates, or First Fruits;[18] of receiving appeals;[19] with the power of subjecting all churches in all parts, to the ecclesiastical discipline of the church of Rome; and lastly, the dispensing Power of the Pope.[20]

11. The Pope's pretended superiority to an Ecumenical Council.

12. The exclusive power of canonizing Saints.

Now, of the twelve abuses here enumerated, it is remarkable that ten, if not eleven, are but expansions of the one grievance—the Papal Power as the centre, and the Pope as the one visible head and sovereign of the Christian church.

The writer next enumerates the personal Instruments, &c. of these abuses: viz.—1. The Cardinals. 2. The excessive number of the Priests and other Ecclesiastics. 3. The Regulars,[21] Mendicant Orders, Jesuits, &c.

Lastly: the means employed by the Papacy to found and preserve its usurped power, namely:—

1. The institution[22] of a Chair of Canon Law, in the university of Bologna, the introduction of Gratian's Canons,[23] and the forged decisions,[24] &c. 2. The prohibition of books, wherever published. 3. The Inquisition. 4. The tremendous power of Excommunication. The two last in their temporal inflictions and consequences equalling, or rather greatly ex-

ceeding, the utmost extent of the punitive power exercised by the temporal sovereign and the civil magistrate, armed with the sword of the criminal law.

It is observable, that the most efficient of all the means adopted by the Roman Pontiffs, viz.—THE CELIBACY OF THE CLERGY, is omitted by this writer: a sufficient proof that he was neither a Protestant nor a *Philosopher*, which in the Italian states, and, indeed, in most Catholic Countries, is the name of Courtesy for an Infidel.

One other remark in justification of the tenet avowed in this chapter, and I shall have said all I deem it necessary to say, on the third form of a Church. That erection of a temporal monarch under the pretence of a spiritual authority, which was not possible in Christendom but by the extinction or entrancement of the spirit of Christianity, and which has therefore been only partially attained by the Papacy—this was effected in full by Mahomet, to the establishment of the most extensive and complete despotism, that ever warred against civilization and the interests of humanity. And had Mahomet retained the name of Christianity, had he deduced his authority from Christ, as his *Principal*, and described his own Caliphate and that of his successors as *vicarious*, there can be no doubt, that to the Mussulman Theocracy, embodied in the different Mahometan dynasties, would belong the name and attributes of Antichrist. But the Prophet of Arabia started out of Paganism an unbaptized Pagan. He was no traitor in the church, but an enemy from without, who levied war against its outward and formal existence, and is, therefore, not chargeable with *apostacy* from a faith, he had never acknowledged, or from a church to which he had never appertained. Neither in the Prophet nor in his system, therefore, can we find the predicted *Anti-Christ, i.e.* a usurped power *in* the church itself, which, in the name of Christ, and pretending his authority, systematically subverts or counteracts the peculiar aims and purposes of Christ's mission; and which, vesting in a mortal his incommunicable headship, destroys (and exchanges for the contrary) the essential contradistinguishing marks or characters of his kingdom on earth.

But apply it, as Wickliffe, Luther,* and indeed all the first Reformers did to the Papacy, and Papal Hierarchy; and we understand at once the grounds of the great apostle's pre-monition, that this Antichrist could not appear till after the dissolution of the Latin empire, and the extinction of the Imperial Power in Rome—and the cause why the Bishop of

* And (be it observed) without any reference to the Apocalypse, the canonical character of which Luther at first rejected, and never cordially received. And without the least sympathy with Luther's suspicions on this head, but on the contrary receiving this sublime poem as the undoubted work of the Apostolic age, and admiring in it the most perfect specimen of symbolic poetry, I am as little disposed to cite it on the present occasion—convinced as I am and hope shortly to convince others, that in the whole series of its magnificent imagery there is not a single symbol, that can be even plausibly interpreted of either the Pope, the Turks, or Napoleon Buonaparte. Of charges not attaching to the moral character, there are few, if any, that I should be more anxious to avoid than that of being an affecter of paradoxes. But the dread of other men's thoughts shall not tempt me to withhold a truth, which the strange errors grounded on the contrary assumption render important. And in the thorough assurance of its truth I make the assertion, that the perspicuity, and (with singularly few exceptions even for *us*) the uniform intelligi-bility, and close consecutive meaning, verse by verse, with the simplicity and grandeur of the plan, and the admirable *ordonnance* of the parts, are among the prominent beauties of the Apocalypse. Nor do I doubt that the substance and main argument of this sacred oratorio, or drama *sui generis* (the Prometheus of Eschylus comes the nearest to *the kind*) were supplied by John the Evangelist: though I incline with Eusebius to find the poet himself in John, an Elder and Contemporary of the Church of Ephesus.[25]

P.S.—It may remove, or at least mitigate the objections to the palliative language in which I have spoken of the doctrines of the Catholic Church, if I remind the Reader that the *Roman* Catholic Church dates its true origin from the Council of Trent.[26] Widely differing from my valued and affectionately respected friend, the Rev. Edward Irving,[27] in his *interpretations* of the Apocalypse and the Book of Daniel, and no less in his *estimation* of the latter, and while I honour his courage, as a Christian minister, almost as much

Constantinople, with all imaginable good wishes and disposition to do the same, could never raise the Patriarchate of the Greek empire into a Papacy. The Bishops of the other Rome became the slaves of the Ottoman, the moment they ceased to be the subjects of the Emperor.

---

as I admire his eloquence as a writer, yet protesting against his somewhat too adventurous speculations on the Persons of the Trinity and the Body of our Lord [28]—I have great delight in extracting (*from his " Sermons, Lectures, and Discourses,*" vol. iii. p. 870) and declaring my cordial assent to the following just observations: viz.—" that *after* the Reformation had taken firmer root, and when God had provided a purer Church, the Council of Trent did corroborate and decree into unalterable laws and constitutions of the Church all those impostures and innovations of the Roman See, which had been in a state of uncertainty, perhaps of permission or even of custom; but which every man till then had been free to testify against, and against which, in fact, there never wanted those in each successive generation who did testify. The Council of Trent *ossified* all those ulcers and blotchers which had deformed the Church, and stamped the hitherto much doubted and controverted prerogative of the Pope with the highest authority recognized in the Church." Then first was the Catholic converted and particularized into the Romish Church, the Church of the Papacy.

No less cordially do I concur with Mr. Irving in his remark in the following page. For I too, "am free to confess and avow moreover, that I believe the soil of the Catholic Church, when Luther arose, was of a stronger mould, fitted to bear forest trees and cedars of God, than the soil of the Protestant Church in the times of Whitfield [29] and Wesley, which (*though sown with the same word*—? *qu.*) hath brought forth only stunted undergrowths, and creeping brushwood." I too, "believe, that the faith of the Protestant Church in Britain had come to a lower ebb, and that it is even now at a lower ebb, than was the faith of the Papal Church when the Spirit of the Lord was able to quicken in it and draw forth of it, such men as Luther, and Melancthon, and Bullenger, Calvin, Bucer,[30] and Latimer, and Ridley, and a score others whom I might name."

And now, as the conclusion of this long note, let me be permitted to add a word or two of Edward Irving himself. That he possesses

We will now proceed to the Second Part, intended as a humble aid to a just appreciation of the measure, which under the auspices of Mr. Peel and the Duke of Wellington is now the Law of the land. This portion of the volume was written while the measure was yet *in prospectu*; before even the particular

---

my unqualified esteem as a man, is only saying, that I know him, and am neither blinded by envy nor bigotry. But my name has been brought into connexion with his, on points that regard his public ministry; and he himself has publicly distinguished me as his friend on public grounds; and in proof of my confidence in his regard, I have not the least apprehension of forfeiting it by a frank declaration of what I think. Well, then! I have no faith in his prophesyings; small sympathy with his fulminations; and in certain peculiarities of his *theological* system, as distinct from his religious principles, I cannot see my way. But I hold withal, and not the less firmly for these discrepancies in our moods and judgments, that EDWARD IRVING possesses more of the spirit and purposes of the first Reformers, that he has more of the Head and Heart, the Life, the Unction, and the genial power of MARTIN LUTHER, than any man now alive; yea, than any man of this and the last century. I see in EDWARD IRVING a minister of Christ after the order of Paul; and if the points, in which I think him either erroneous, or excessive and *out of bounds*, have been at any time a subject of serious regret with me, this regret has arisen principally or altogether from the apprehension of their narrowing the sphere of his influence, from the too great probability that they may furnish occasion or pretext for withholding or withdrawing many from those momentous truths, which the age especially needs, and for the enforcement of which he hath been so highly and especially gifted! Finally, my friend's intellect is too instinct with life, too *potential* to remain stationary; and assuming, as every satisfied believer must be supposed to do, the truth of my own views, I look forward with confident hope to a time when his soul shall have perfected her victory over the dead letter of the senses and its apparitions in the sensuous understanding; when the Halycon IDEAS shall have alit on the surging sea of his conceptions,

> "Which then shall quite forget to rave,
> While Birds of Calm sit brooding on the charmed wave."
>
> MILTON.[31]

123

clauses of the Bill were made public. It was written to explain and vindicate the author's refusal to sign a Petition against any change in the scheme of Law and Policy established at the Revolution. But as the arguments are in no respect affected by this circumstance; nay, as their constant reference to, and dependence on, one fixed General Principle, which will at once explain both why the author finds the actual Bill so much less

---

But to return from the *Personal*, for which I have little taste at any time, and the contrary when it stands in any connection with myself ————in order to the removal of one main impediment to the spiritual resuscitation of Protestantism, it seems to me indispensable, that in freedom and unfearing faith, with that courage which cannot but flow from the inward and life-like assurance, "that neither death, nor things present nor things to come, nor heighth, nor depth, nor any other creature, shall be able to separate us from the love of God, which is in Christ Jesus our Lord"—(Rom. viii. 38, 39)—the rulers of our Churches and our teachers of theology should meditate and draw the obvious, though perhaps unpalatable, inferences from the following two or three plain truths:—First, that Christ, "the Spirit of Truth," [32] has promised to be with his Church even to the end. Secondly: that Christianity was described as a Tree to be raised from the Seed, so described by Him who brought the Seed from Heaven and first sowed it.[33] Lastly: that in the process of Evolution, there are in every plant growths of transitory use and duration. "The integuments of the seed, having fulfilled their destined office of protection, burst and decay. After the leaves have unfolded, the Cotyledons, that had performed their functions, wither and drop off." * The husk is a genuine growth of "The Staff of Life"; yet we must separate it from the grain. It is, therefore, the cowardice of faithless superstition, if we stand in greater awe of the palpable interpolations of vermin; if we shrink from the removal of excrescences that contain nothing of nobler parentage than maggots of moth or chafer. Let us cease to confound oak-apples with acorns; still less, though gilded by the fashion of the day, let us mistake them for Golden Pippins or Renates.†

* Smith's Introduction to Botany.[34]
† The fruit from a Pippin grafted on a Pippin, is called a Rennet, *i.e.*, Renate (re-natus) or twice-born.

objectionable than he had feared, and yet so much less complete and satisfactory than he had wished, will be rendered more striking by the reader's consciousness that the arguments were suggested by no wish or purpose either of attacking or supporting any particular measure: it has not been thought necessary or advisable to alter the form. Nay, if the author be right in his judgment, that the Bill lately passed, if characterized by its own contents and capabilities, really *is*—with or without any such intention on the part of its framers—a STEPPING-STONE, and nothing more; whether to the subversion or to the more perfect establishment of the Constitution in Church and State, must be determined by other causes; the Bill in itself is equally fit for either—*Tros Tyriusve*,[35] it offers the same facilities of transit to both, though with a foreclosure to the first comer.—If this be a right, as it is the author's sincere judgment and belief, there is a propriety in retaining the language of anticipation. Mons adhuc parturit: the "ridiculus Mus" was but an omen.[36]

1. 'It is not the Catholic Church as such that I attack, but Popery, built as it is on lies, implanted by the most abominable of despotisms, contrary to Christ's law and His inalienable mandate, and jeopardizing the peace and security of every Church and State'. Quotation untraced; the sentence does not appear either in the first or in the second edition of Spanzotti's *Disordini Morali e Politici* &c., referred to by Coleridge below, p. 118.
2. Book V, Sect. iii (pt. 1), para. 63.
3. For the composition, numbers, and beliefs of the High Church Party in the early nineteenth century, see J. H. Overton, *The English Church in the Nineteenth Century: 1800–1833* (London, 1894).
4. Quotation untraced; it appears to refer to the seventeenth-century dispute concerning article XIX of the Church of England: '. . . the Church of Rome hath erred, not only in [its] living and manner of Ceremonies, but also in matters of Faith.'
5. See (e.g.) Burigni, *Life of Grotius* (London, 1754), p. 288;

letters by Leibniz, in Rommel, *Leibniz und Landgraf*, &c. (Frankfurt-am-Main, 1847) I. 284ff; II. 19.

6. Wyclif anticipated Luther's identification of Pope with the antichrist in a number of writings, e.g. 'Of Antecrist and his Meynee', in *Three Treatises on the Church*, 1384, ed. Todd (Dublin, 1851).

7. Matthew x. 34.

8. More usually *Summa Theologica*.

9. Antoine Arnauld (1612–94), Jansenist theologian; Jacques Benigne Bossuet (1627–1704), Bishop of Meaux, notoriously persuasive Catholic apologist.

10. 'What must be done, and what must be believed.'

11. Leo X excommunicated Luther in 1520.

12. The liberal wing of Protestantism (which followed Jacobus Arminius, 1560–1609, and Hugo Grotius, 1583–1645), opposed to Calvinism on the questions especially of free-will and conciliation with Rome.

13. The papal tiara.

14. Milan 1797–8.

15. The followers of the Albigensian heresy were for the most part wiped out by the elder de Montfort in a campaign of great cruelty (1208–18), and finished off by the Dominican Inquisition. In 1209 Innocent III instituted a crusade against the Waldenses, or Vaudois, pockets of whom survived, however, to be persecuted as late as the seventeenth century.

16. i.e., after the split (1054) between the Eastern and Western Churches.

17. The most important cases in the ecclesiastical courts.

18. The first year's revenue of an ecclesiastical benefice, paid to the Papal Curia.

19. i.e., from the lower ecclesiastical courts.

20. The power to license an act otherwise canonically illegal.

21. Priests living within a community, as distinguished from secular priests living in society.

22. *c.* 1100.

23. Gratian (died *c.* 1179), 'the father of Canon Law'; his *Decretum* (a systematic collection of conciliar decrees, papal pronouncements, &c.) was published *c.* 1140, and adopted later as the first part of the Corpus of Canon Law.

24. A collection of documents in Canon Law, many of them

spurious, put together to defend (among other things) the episcopal supremacy of the Pope.

25. Eusebius, *Ecclesiastical History*, III. 23.
26. The decisions of the Council of Trent (which among other things curtailed the power of the metropolitan bishops over their suffragans, and in doing so greatly reinforced the Pope's episcopal supremacy) were confirmed by the Bull 'Benedictus Deus' in 1564.
27. Edward Irving (1792–1834), founder of the 'Catholic Apostolic Church'.
28. Coleridge's protests will be found in the marginalia to his copy of Irving's *Sermons*, &c. (London, 1828) in the British Museum.
29. George Whitfield (1714–70), Calvinist-Methodist preacher, contemporary of Wesley.
30. Philipp Melanchthon (1497–1560); Johann Heinrich Bullenger (1504–75), Martin Bucer (1491–1551), Protestant reformers; Irving's 'Knox' replaced by Bucer in all editions of *Church and State*.
31. 'On the Morning of Christ's Nativity', ll. 67–8.
32. See John xiv. 17; xv. 26; xvi. 13.
33. Matthew xiii. 32; Luke xiii. 19.
34. James E. Smith, *An Introduction to Physiological and Systematical Botany* (London, 1807), pp. 94, 97.
35. *Aeneid* I. 574.
36. A reference to Horace, *Ars Poetica*, 139, 'the mountains will be in travail, and an absurd little mouse be born'.

SECOND PART:

OR,

AIDS TO A RIGHT APPRECIATION

OF

THE BILL

ADMITTING CATHOLICS TO SIT IN BOTH HOUSES
OF PARLIAMENT, &c. &c.

'Αμέλει μὰ τὸν Δί' οὐκ ἐνασπιδώσομαι,
Λέξω δ' ὑπὲρ Ἑτερογνωμόνων, ἅ μοι δοκεῖ·
Καίτοι δέδοικα πολλά· τούς τε γὰρ τρόπους
Τοὺς ξυμπολίτων οἶδα χαίροντας σφόδρα
'Εάν τις αὐτοὺς εὐλογῇ καὶ τὴν πόλιν,
'Ανὴρ ἀλαζὼν, καὶ δίκαια κἄδικα·
Κἀνταῦθα λανθάνουσ' ἀπεμπολώμενοι.

'ΑΡΙΣΤΟΦ. 'Αχαρνῆς. 367.[1]

TO A FRIEND.

Yes, Sir, I estimate the beauty and benefit of what you have called 'A harmony in fundamentals, and a conspiration in the constituent parts of the Body Politic,' as highly as the sturdiest zealot for the petition, which I have declined to subscribe. If I met a man, who should deny that an imperium in imperio was in itself an evil, I would not attempt to reason with him: he is too ignorant. Or if, conceding this, he should deny that the Romish Priesthood in Ireland does in fact constitute an *imperium in imperio*, I yet would not argue the matter with him: for he must be a Bigot. But my objection to the argument is, that it is nothing to the purpose. And even so, with regard to the arguments grounded on the dangerous errors and superstitions of the Romish Church. They may be all very true; but they are nothing to the purpose. Without any loss they might *pair off* with 'the Heroes of Trafalgar and Waterloo,' and 'our Catholic ancestors, to whom we owe our Magna Charta,' on the other side. If the *prevention* of an evil were the point in question, *then* indeed! But the day of prevention has long past by. The evil exists: and neither rope, sword, nor sermon, neither suppression nor conversion, can remove it. Not that I think slightingly of the last; but even those who hope more sanguinely, than I can pretend to do respecting the effects ultimately to result from the labours of missionaries, the dispersion of controversial tracts, and whatever other lawful means and implements it may be in our power to employ—even these must admit that if the remedy could cope with the magnitude and inveteracy of the disease, it is wholly inadequate to the urgency of the symptoms. In this instance it would be no easy matter to take the horse to the water; and the rest of the proverb you know. But why do I waste words? There is and can be but one question: and there is and can be but one way of stating it. A great numerical majority of the inhabitants of one integral *part* of the realm profess a religion hostile to that professed by the majority of the whole realm: and a religion, too, which the latter regard, and have had good reason to regard, as equally hostile to liberty, and the sacred rights of conscience generally. In fewer words, three-fourths of His Majesty's Irish subjects are Roman Catholics, with a papal priesthood, while three-fourths of the sum total of his Majesty's subjects are Protestants. This with its causes and consequences is the evil. It is not in our power, by any immediate or direct means, to effect its removal. The point, therefore, to be determined is: Will the measures now in contemplation be likely to diminish or to aggravate it? And to the determination of this point on the probabilities suggested by reason and experience, I would gladly be aidant, as far as my poor mite of judgment will enable me.

Let us, however, first discharge what may well be deemed a debt of justice from every well educated Protestant to his Catholic fellow-subjects of the Sister Island. At least, let us ourselves understand the true cause of the evil as it now exists. To what, and to whom is the present state of Ireland mainly to be attributed? This should be the question: and to this I answer aloud, that it is mainly attributable to those, who during a period of little less than a whole century used as a *Substitute* what Providence had given into their hand as an *Opportunity*; who chose to consider as *superseding* the most sacred duty a code of law, that could have been excused only on the plea, that it enabled them to perform it! To the sloth and improvidence, the weakness and wickedness, of the gentry, clergy, and governors of Ireland, who persevered in preferring intrigue, violence, and selfish expatriation to a system of preventive and remedial measures, the efficacy of which had been warranted for them by the whole provincial history of ancient Rome, *cui pacare* subactos summa erat sapientia; [2] warranted for them by the happy results of the few exceptions to the contrary scheme unhappily pursued by their and our ancestors.

I can imagine no work of genius that would more appropriately decorate the dome or wall of a Senate house, than an abstract of Irish history from the landing of Strongbow [3] to the battle of the Boyne, or a yet later period, embodied in intelligible emblems—an allegorical history-piece designed in the spirit of a Rubens of a Buonarroti, and with the wild lights, portentous shades, and saturated colours of a Rembrandt, Caravaggio, and Spagnoletti. [4] To complete the great moral and political lesson by the historic contrast, nothing more would be required, than by some equally effective means to possess the mind of the spectator with the state and condition of ancient Spain, at less than half a century from the final conclusion of an obstinate and almost unremitting conflict of two hundred years by Agrippa's subjugation of the Cantabrians, [5] omnibus Hispaniæ populis devictis et *pacatis*. [6] At the breaking up of the empire, the West Goths conquered the country and made division of the lands. Then came eight centuries of Moorish domination. Yet so deeply had Roman wisdom impressed the fairest characters of the Roman mind, that at this very hour, if we except a comparatively insignificant portion of Arabic Derivatives, the natives throughout the whole peninsula speak a language less differing from the Romana Rustica, or Provincial Latin, of the times of Lucan and Seneca, than any two of its dialects from each other. The time approaches, I trust, when our political economists may study the science of the *provincial* policy of the ancients in detail, under the auspices of hope, for immediate and practical purposes.

In my own mind I am persuaded, that the necessity of the penal and precautionary statutes passed under Elizabeth [7] and the three succeeding reigns, is to be found as much in the passions and prejudices of the one party, as in the dangerous dispositions of the other. The best excuse for this cruel code is the imperfect knowledge and mistaken maxims common to both parties. It is only to a limited extent, that laws can be wiser than the nation for which they are enacted. The annals of the first five or six centuries of the Hebrew nation in Palestine present an almost continued history of disobedience, of laws broken or utterly lost sight of, of maxims violated, and schemes of consummate wisdom left unfulfilled. Even a yet diviner seed must be buried and undergo an apparent corruption before—at a late period—it shot up and could appear in its own kind. In our judgments respecting *actions* we must be guided by the idea, but in applying the rule to the *agents*, by comparison. To speak gently of our forefathers is at once piety and policy. Nor let it be forgotten, that only by making the detection of their errors the occasion of our own wisdom, do we acquire a right to censure them at all.

Whatever may be thought of the settlement that followed the battle of the Boyne and the extinction of the war in Ireland, yet when this had been made and submitted to, it would have been the far wiser policy, I doubt not, to have provided for the safety of the Constitution by improving the quality of the elective franchise, leaving the eligibility open, or like the former limited only by considerations of property. Still, however, the scheme of exclusion and disqualification had its plausible side.[8] The ink was scarcely dry on the parchment-rolls and proscription-lists of the Popish parliament.[9] The crimes of the man were generalized into attributes of his faith; and the Irish Catholics collectively were held accomplices in the perfidy and baseness of the king. Alas! his immediate adherents had afforded too great colour to the charge. The Irish massacre [10] was in the mouth of every Protestant, not as an event to be remembered, but as a thing of recent expectation, fear still blending with the sense of deliverance. At no time, therefore, could the disqualifying system have been enforced with so little reclamation of the conquered party, or with so little outrage on the general feeling of the country. There was no time, when it was so capable of being indirectly useful as a *sedative* in order to the application of the remedies directly indicated, or as a counter-power reducing to inactivity whatever disturbing forces might have interfered with their operation. And *had* this use been made of these exclusive laws, and had they been enforced as the precursors and negative conditions, but above all as *bonâ fide* accompaniments of a process of *emancipation*, properly and worthily so named, the code would at this day have been remembered in Ireland only as when recalling a dangerous fever of our boyhood we think of the nauseous drugs and drenching-horn, and congratulate ourselves that our doctors now-a-days know how to manage these things less coarsely. But this angry code was neglected as an opportunity, and mistaken for a *substitute*: et hinc illæ lacrymæ![11]

And at this point I find myself placed again in connection with the main question, and which I contend to be the pertinent question, *viz.*, The evil being admitted, and its immediate removal impossible, is the admission of Catholics into both Houses of Legislature likely to mitigate or to aggravate it? And here the problem is greatly narrowed by the fact, that no man pretends to regard this admissibility as a *direct* remedy, or specific antidote for the diseases, under which Ireland labours. No! it is to act, we are told, as introductory to the direct remedies. In short, this Emancipation is to be, like the penal code which it repeals, a *sedative*, though in the opposite form of an anodyne cordial, that will itself be entitled to the name of a remedial measure in proportion as it shall be found to render the body susceptible of the more direct remedies that are to follow. Its object is to tranquillize Ireland. Safety, peace, and good neighbourhood, influx of capital, diminution of absentee-ism, industrious habits, and a long train of blessings will follow. But the indispensable condition, the *causa causarum et causa-torum*,[12] is general tranquillity. Such is the language held by all the more intelligent advocates and encomiasts of Emancipation. The sense of the question therefore is, will the measure tend to produce tranquillity?

Now it is evident, that there are two parties to be satisfied, and that the measure is likely to effect this purpose according as it is calculated to satisfy reasonable men of both. Reasonable men are easily satisfied: would they were as numerous as they are pacable! We must, however, understand the word comparatively, as including all those on both sides, who by their superior information, talents, or property, are least likely to be under the dominion of vulgar antipathies, and who may be rationally expected to influence (and in certain cases, and in alliance with a vigorous government, to over-rule) the feelings and sentiments of the rest.

Now the two indispensable conditions under which alone the measure can permanently satisfy the reasonable, that is, the *satisfiable*, of both parties, supposing that in both parties such men exist, and that they form the influencive class in both, are these. First, that the Bill for the repeal of the exclusive statutes, and the admission of Catholics to the full privileges of British subjects, shall be grounded on some determinate PRINCIPLE, which involving interests and duties common to both parties as British subjects, both parties may be expected to recognize, and required to maintain inviolable. Second, that this principle shall contain in itself an evident definite and unchangeable *boundary*, a line of demarcation, a *ne plus ultra*, which in all reasonable men and lovers of their country shall preclude the *wish* to pass beyond it, and extinguish the hope of so doing in such as are neither.

But though the measure should be such as to satisfy all reasonable men, still it is possible that the number and influence of these may not be sufficient to leaven the mass, or to over-rule the agitators. I admit this; but instead of weakening what I have here said, it affords an additional argument in its favour. For if an argument satisfactory to the reasonable part should nevertheless fail in securing tranquillity, still less can the result be expected from an arbitrary adjustment that can satisfy no part. If a measure grounded on principle, and possessing the character of an ultimatum should still, through the prejudices and passions of one or of both parties, fail of success, it would be folly to expect it from a measure that left full scope and sphere to those passions; which kept alive the fears of the one party, while it sharpened the cupidity of the other. With confidence, therefore, I re-assert, that only by reference to a principle, possessing the characters above enumerated, can any satisfactory measure be framed, and that if this should fail in producing the tranquillity aimed at, it will be in vain sought in any other.

Again, it is evident that no principle can be appropriate to such a measure, which does not bear directly on the evil to be removed or mitigated. Consequently, it should be our first business to discover in what this evil truly and essentially consists. It is, we know, a compound of many ingredients. But we want to ascertain what the *base* is, that communicates the quality of evil, of *political* evil, of evil which it is the duty of a *statesman* to guard against, to various other ingredients, which without the base would have been innoxious: or though evils in themselves, yet evils of such a kind, as to be counted by all wise statesmen among the tares, which must be suffered to grow up with the wheat to the close of the harvest, and left for the Lord of the Harvest to separate.

Further: the principle, the grounding and directing principle of an effectual enactment, must be one, on which a Catholic might consistently vindicate and recommend the measure to Catholics. It must therefore be independent of all differences purely theological. And the facts and documents, by which the truth and practical importance of the principle are to be proved or illustrated, should be taken by preference from periods anterior to the division of the Latin Church into Romish and Protestant. It should be such, in short, that an orator might with strict historical propriety introduce the Framers and Extorters of Magna Charta pleading to their Catholic descendants in behalf of the measure grounded on such a Principle, and invoking them in the name of the Constitution, over whose growth *they* had kept armed watch, and by the sacred obligation to maintain it which they had entailed on their posterity.

This is the condition under which alone I could conscientiously vote, and which being fulfilled, I should most zealously vote for the admission of Lay Catholics, not only to both houses of the Legislature, but to all other offices below the Crown, without any exception.[13] Moreover, in the fulfilment of this condition, in the solemn recognition and establishment of a Principle having the characters here specified, I find the only necessary security—convinced, that this, if acceded to by the Catholic Body, would in effect be such, and that any other security will either be hollow, or frustrate the purpose of the Bill.

Now this condition would be fulfilled, the required Principle would be given, provided that the law for the repeal of the sundry statutes affecting the Catholics were introduced by, and grounded on, a declaration, to which every possible character of solemnity should be given, that at no time and under no circumstances has it ever been, nor can it ever be, compatible with the spirit or consistent with the safety of the British Constitution, to recognize in the Roman Catholic Priesthood, as now constituted, a component Estate of the realm, or persons capable, individually or collectively, of becoming the Trustees and usufructuary Proprietors of that elective and circulative property, originally reserved for the permanent maintenance of the National Church. And further, it is expedient that the Preamble of the Bill should expressly declare and set forth, that this exclusion of the Members of the Romish Priesthood (comprehending all under oaths of canonical obedience to the Pope as their ecclesiastical sovereign) from the trusts and offices of the National Church, and from all participation in the proceeds of the Nationalty, is enacted and established on grounds wholly irrelative to any doctrines received and taught by the Romish Church as Articles of Faith, and protested against as such by the Churches of the Reformation; but that it is enacted on grounds derived and inherited from our ancestors before the Reformation, and by them maintained and enforced to the fullest extent that the circumstances of the times permitted, with no other exceptions and interruptions than those effected by fraud, or usurpation, or foreign force, or the temporary fanaticism of the meaner sort.

In what manner the enactment of this principle shall be effected, is of comparatively small importance, provided it be distinctly set forth as that great constitutional *security*, the known existence of which is the ground and condition of the *right* of the Legislature to dispense with other less essential safe-guards of the constitution, not unnecessary, perhaps, at the time of their enactment, but of temporary and accidental necessity. The form, I repeat, the particular mode in which the principle shall be recognized, the security established, is comparatively indifferent. Let it only be understood first, as the provision, by the retention of which the Legislature possess a moral and constitutional right to make the change in question; as that, the known existence of which permits the law to *ignore* the Roman Catholics under any other name than that of British subjects; and secondly, as the express condition, the basis of a virtual compact between the claimants and the nation, which condition cannot be broken or evaded without subverting (morally) the articles and clauses founded thereon.

N.B.—I do not assert that the provision here stated *is* an absolute security. My positions are,—first, that it may with better reason and more probability be proposed as such, than any other hitherto devised; secondly, that no other securities can supersede the expediency and necessity of this, but that this will greatly diminish or altogether remove the necessity of any other: further, that without this the present measure cannot be rationally expected to produce that tranquillity, which it is the aim and object of the framers to bring about; and lastly, that the necessity of the declaration, as above given, formally and solemnly to be made and recorded, is not evacuated by this pretext, that no one intends to transfer the Church Establishment to the Romish Priesthood, or to divide it with them.

One thing, however, is of importance, that I should premise —namely, that the existing state of the Elective Franchise * in

* Though by the Bill which is now Law, the Forty Shilling Free-holders no longer possess the elective franchise,[14] yet as this particular clause of the Bill already has been, and may hereafter be, made a pretext for agitation, the following paragraph has been retained, in the belief, that its moral uses have not been altogether superseded by the retraction of this most unhappy boon.

Ireland, in reference to the fatal present of the Union Ministry to the Landed Interest,[15] that the true Deianira Shirt of the Irish Hercules,[16] is altogether excluded from the theme and purpose of this disquisition. It ought to be considered by the Legislature, abstracted from the creed professed by the great majority of these nominal Freeholders. The recent abuse of the influence resulting from this profession should be regarded as an accidental aggravation of the mischief, that displayed rather than constituted its malignity. It is even desirable, that it should be preserved separate from the Catholic Question, and in no necessary dependence on the fate of the Bill now on the eve of presentation to Parliament. Whether this be carried or be lost, it will still remain a momentous question, urgently calling for the decision of the Legislature—whether the said extension of the elective franchise has not introduced an uncombining and wholly incongruous ingredient into the representative system, irreconcilable with the true principle of election, and virtually disfranchising the class, to whom, on every ground of justice and of policy, the right unquestionably belongs—under *any* circumstances overwhelming the voices of the rest of the community; in *ordinary* times concentering in the great Land-owners a virtual monopoly of the elective power; and in times of factious excitement depriving them even of their natural and rightful influence.[17]

These few suggestions on the expediency of revising the state of the representation in Ireland are, I am aware, but a digression from the main subject of the Chapter. But this in fact is already completed, as far as my purpose is concerned. The reasons on which the necessity of the proposed declaration is grounded, have been given at large in the former part of the volume. Here, therefore, I should end; but that I anticipate two objections, of sufficient force to deserve a comment, and form the matter of a concluding paragraph.

First, it may be objected, that after abstracting the portion of evil, that may be plausibly attributed to the peculiar state of landed property in Ireland, there are evils directly resulting from the Romanism of the most numerous class of the Inhabitants, besides that of an extra-national priesthood, and against the political consequences of which the above declaration provides no security. To this I reply, that as no bridge ever did or can possess the demonstrable perfections of the mathematical arch, so can no existing state adequately correspond to the *idea* of a state. In nations and governments the most happily constituted, there will be deformities and obstructions, peccant humours and irregular actions, which affect indeed the *perfection* of the state, but not its essential forms; which retard, but do not necessarily prevent its progress: casual disorders, which though they aggravate the *growing pains* of a nation, may yet, by the vigorous counteraction which they excite, even promote its *growth*. Inflammations in the extremities, and unseemly boils on the surface, dare not be confounded with exhaustive misgrowths, or the poison of a false life in the vital organs. Nay, and this remark is of special pertinency to our present purpose— even where the former derive a malignant character from their co-existence with the latter, yet the wise physician will direct his whole attention to the *constitutional* ailments, knowing that when the source, the fons et fomes veneni,[18] is sealed up, the accessories will either dry up of themselves, or, returning to their natural character rank among the infirmities, which flesh is heir to; and either admit of a gradual remedy, or where this is impracticable, or when the medicine would be worse than the disease, are to be endured, as *tolerabiles* ineptiæ,[19] trials of patience, and occasions of charity. We have here had the state chiefly in view; but the Protestant will to little purpose have availed himself of his free access to the Scriptures, will have read at least the Epistles of St. Paul, with a very unthinking spirit, who does not apply the same maxims to the church of Christ, who has yet to learn, that the church militant is "a floor whereon wheat and chaff are mingled together;"[20] that even grievous evils and errors may exist that do not concern the nature or being of a church, and that they may even prevail in the particular church, to which we belong, without justifying a separation from the same, and without invalidating its claims on our affection as a true and living part of the Church Universal.

And with regard to such evils we must adopt the advice that Augustine (a man not apt to offend by any excess of charity) gave to the complainers of his day—ut misericorditer corripiant quod possunt, quod non possunt patienter ferant, et cum dilectione lugeant, donec aut emendet Deus aut in messe eradicet zizania et paleas ventilet.[21]

Secondly, it may be objected that the declaration, so peremptorily by me required is altogether unnecessary, that no one thinks of alienating the church property, directly or indirectly, that there is no intention of recognising the Romish Priests in law, by entitling them as such, to national maintenance, or in the language of the day, by taking them into the pay of the state. In short, that the National Church is no more in danger than the Christian. And is this the opinion, the settled judgment, of one who has studied the signs of the times? Can the person who makes these assertions, have ever read a pamphlet by Mr. Secretary Croker? [22] Or the surveys of the Counties, published under the authority of the now extinct Board of Agriculture? [23] Or has he heard, or attentively perused the successive debates in both Houses during the late agitation of the Catholic Question? [24] If he have—why then, relatively to the objector, and to as many as entertain the same opinions, my reply is:—the objection is unanswerable.

1. 'By Zeus, I certainly shan't skulk behind my shield—I shall speak my mind on behalf of those who think differently. And yet I'm much afraid—for I know the moods of my fellow-citizens, who are delighted if some quack praises them and their city, whether he's right or wrong—and it's then they don't notice that they're being bought and sold.' Aristophanes, *Acharnians*, 367f., altered.
2. 'whose greatest wisdom was to *pacify* those she had subdued'.
3. Richard de Clare, or Richard Strongbow (d. 1176), whose invasion of Ireland in 1170 (probably at Henry II's instigation) is usually regarded as the first English interference in Irish History.

4. Jusepe Ribera (1591–1652), Spanish painter living in Naples, and there nicknamed 'lo Spagnoletto'.
5. See Dio Cassius's *Roman History*, LIV. 11.
6. 'all the peoples of Spain utterly defeated and *pacified*'.
7. The Acts of Uniformity and Supremacy, 1559.
8. By a series of acts passed in the early years of William and Mary Catholics in Ireland were deprived of almost all civil rights; they were excluded from the elective franchise and from the professions, and those who were not already disqualified from owning land (by the Act of Settlement, 1660) were prohibited from acquiring it.
9. The Parliament summoned by James II in Ireland in 1689; it consisted almost wholly of Catholics, and passed the Act of Attainder, by which some 2000 'attainted' Protestants were to be tried for High Treason.
10. i.e., of English and Scottish Protestants at the start of the Ulster Rebellion, 1641.
11. 'and hence those tears', Terence, *Andreia*, I. i. 99.
12. 'the cause of causes and of effects'.
13. By section 12 of the 1829 Act the offices of Lord Chancellor, Lord Keeper of the Great Seal, Lord Lieutenant of Ireland etc., were still closed to Catholics.
14. In 1829 the property-qualification was raised from 40 shillings to £10.
15. The Landed Interest in Ireland usually managed to induce by one means or another the 'forty-shilling freeholders' (enfranchised 1793) to vote for them, so that by far the greater number of Irish MPs after the Union were representatives of the landowning classes.
16. Hercules burned himself to death after putting on a poisoned shirt made for him by his wife Deianira, which corroded his flesh and could not be removed.
17. In 1826, by the influence of O'Connell's Catholic Association, many forty-shilling freeholders voted for emancipationist candidates, several of whom were returned at the expense of the representatives of the Landed Interest.
18. 'the fountain and tinder of the poison'.
19. 'absurdities which can be tolerated'. Calvin, 'Anglis Francfordiensibus', *Opera* XV. 394, in *Corpus Reformatorum*.
20. cf. Matthew iii. 12.

21. 'Let them tenderly castigate what they can; what they cannot, bear patiently; and complain with love, until God either puts things right, or roots out the tares that are in his crop, and winnows away the chaff'; *Contra Epistolam Parmeniani*, III. ii. 5 (Migne *PL*, XLIII, 94); all editions have *delectione* ('choice'), for *dilectione*, surely an unintentional alteration.

22. J. W. Croker (1780–1857), literary critic and Tory politician, had proposed in *A Sketch of the State of Ireland*, (1808), pp. 45–6, that tithes be replaced in Ireland by 'a poundage upon all rents', by which would be supported not only the Protestant, but the Catholic, clergy.

23. The Board of Agriculture was founded in 1793 and abolished in 1822; the Board published two series of county reports between 1793 and 1813; Coleridge refers to the reporters' hostility towards tithes.

24. Wellington's cabinet discussed in 1828 the possibility (also considered by Pitt at the time of the Union) of granting state salaries to Catholic priests, in exchange for Catholic acceptance of 'securities' (see above, p. 12, note 3); the plan was dropped as impossible to get through Parliament.

GLOSSARY

TO THE APPENDED LETTER.

As all my readers are not bound to understand Greek, and yet, according to *my* deepest convictions, the truths set forth in the following Combat of Wit, between the Man of Reason and the Man of the Senses have an interest for all, I have been induced to prefix the explanations of the few Greek words, and words minted from the Greek:

Cosmos—world. Toutos cosmos [1]—*this* world. Heteros— the other, in the sense of opposition to, or discrepancy with some former; as Heterodoxy, in opposition to Orthodoxy. Allos—an other, simply and without precluding or superseding the one before mentioned. Allocosmite—a Denizen of another world.

Mystes, from the Greek μύω—one who *muses* with closed lips, as meditating on *Ideas* which may indeed be suggested and awakened, but cannot, like the images of sense and the conceptions of the understanding, be adequately *expressed* by words.

N.B.—Where a person mistakes the anomalous misgrowths of his own individuality for ideas, or truths of universal reason, he may, without impropriety, be called a *Mystic*, in the abusive sense of the term; though pseudo-mystic, or phantast, would be the more proper designation. Heraclitus, Plato, Bacon, Leibnitz, were Mystics, in the primary sense of the term: Iamblichus,[2] and his successors, Phantasts.

῎Επεα ζώοντα [3]—living words.—The following words from Plato may be Englished: "the commune and the dialect of Gods w th, or toward men;" [4] and those attributed to Pythagoras:

"the verily subsistent numbers or powers, the most prescient (or provident) principles of the Earth and the Heavens." [5]

And here, though not falling under the leading title, Glossary, yet, as tending to the same object that of fore-arming the reader for the following dialogue, I transcribe two or three annotations, which I had *penciled*, (for the book was lent to me by a friend who had himself borrowed it) on the margins of a volume, recently published, and entitled, "The Natural History of Enthusiasm." [6] They will, at least, remind some of my old school-fellows of the habit, for which I was even then noted: and for others they may serve, as a specimen of the Marginalia, which, if brought together from the various books, my own and those of a score others, would go near to form as bulky a volume as most of those old folios, through which the larger portion of them are dispersed.

HISTORY OF ENTHUSIASM.

I

"Whatever is practically important on religion or morals, may at all times be advanced and argued in the simplest terms of colloquial expression."—p. 21.

NOTE.

I do not believe this. Be it so, however. But why? Simply, because, the terms and phrases of the Theological Schools have, by their continual iteration from the pulpit, *become* colloquial. The science of one age becomes the common sense of a succeeding. (See Aids to Reflection, pp. 7–11; but especially at the note at p. 252.) The author adds—"from the pulpit, perhaps, no other style should at any time be heard." Now I can conceive no more direct means of depriving Christianity of one of its peculiar attributes, that of enriching and enlarging the mind, *while* it purifies, and in the very *act* of purifying, the will and affections, than the maxim here prescribed by the historian of Enthusiasm. From the intensity of commercial life in this country, and from some other less creditable causes, there is found even among our better educated men, a vagueness in the use of words, which presents, indeed, no obstacle to the intercourse of the market, but is absolutely incompatible with the attainment or communication of distinct and precise conceptions. Hence in every department of exact knowledge, a peculiar nomenclature is indispensable. The Anatomist, Chemist, Botanist, Mineralogist, yea, even the common artizan, and the rude Sailor, discover that "the terms of colloquial expression," are too general and too lax to answer *their* purposes: and on what grounds can the science of self-knowledge, and of our relations to God and our own spirits, be presumed to form an exception? Every new term expressing a fact, or a difference, not precisely and adequately expressed by any other word in the same language, is a new organ of thought for the mind that has learnt it.

II

"The region of abstract conceptions, of lofty reasonings, has an atmosphere too subtle to support the health of true piety.— In accordance with this, the Supreme *in his word* reveals barely a glimpse of his essential glories. By some naked affirmations we are, indeed, secured against grovelling notions of the divine nature; but *these hints are incidental, and so scanty, that every excursive mind goes far beyond them in its conception of the Infinite Attributes*."—p. 26.

NOTE.

By abstract conceptions the author means what I should call *Ideas*, which as such I contradistinguish from conceptions, whether abstracted or generalized. But it is with his *meaning*, not with his terms, that I am at present concerned. Now that the *personëity* of God, the idea of God as the I AM, is presented more prominently in Scripture, than the (so called) physical attributes, is most true; and forms one of the distinctive characters of its superior worth and value. It was by dwelling

147

too exclusively on the Infinites, that the ancient Greek Philosophers, Plato excepted, fell into Pantheism, as in later times did Spinosa. *I forbid you*, says Plato, *to call God the Infinite! If you dare name him at all, say rather the Measure of Infinity.*[7] Nevertheless, it would be easy to place *in synopsi* before the author such a series of Scripture passages, as would incline him to retract his assertion. The Eternal, the Omnipresent, the Omniscient, the one absolute Good, the Holy, the Living, the Creator as well as Former of the Universe, the Father of Spirits —can the author's mind go *far* beyond these? Yet these are all clearly affirmed of the Supreme ONE in the Scriptures.

III

The following pages from p. 26 to p. 36 contain a succession of eloquent and splendid paragraphs on the celestial orders, and the expediency or necessity of their being concealed from us, lest we should receive such overwhelming conceptions of the divine greatness as to render us incapable of devotion and prayer on the Scripture model. "Were it," says the eloquent writer, "indeed permitted to man to gaze upwards from step to step, and from range to range of these celestial hierarchies, to the lowest steps of the Eternal Throne, what liberty of heart would afterwards be left him in drawing near to the Father of Spirits?" But the substance of these pages will be found implied in the following reply to them.

NOTE.

More weight with me than all this Pelion upon Ossa of imaginary Hierarchies has the single remark of Augustine, there neither are nor can be but three essential differences of Being, viz. the Absolute, the Rational Finite, and the Finite irrational; i.e. God, Man, and Brute![8] Besides, the whole scheme is unscriptural, if not contra-scriptural. Pile up winged Hierarchies on Hierarchies, and outblaze the Cabalists,[9] and Dionysius the Areopagite;[10] yet what a gaudy vapor for a healthful mind is the whole conception (or rather Phantasm) compared with the awful Hope held forth in the Gospel, to be one with God in and through the Mediator Christ, even the living, co-eternal Word and Son of God!

But through the whole of this eloquent Declamation, I find two errors predominate, and both, it appears to me, dangerous errors. First, that the rational and consequently the only true Ideas of the Supreme Being, *are* incompatible with the spirit of prayer and petitionary pleading taught and exemplified in the Scriptures. Second, that this *being* the case, and "supplication with arguments and importunate requests" *being* irrational and *known* by the Supplicant to be such, it is nevertheless a duty to pray in this fashion. In other words, it is asserted that the Supreme Being requires of his rational creatures, as the condition of their offering acceptable worship to him, that they should wilfully blind themselves to the light, which he had himself given them, as the contradistinguishing character of their Humanity, without which they could not pray to him at all; and that drugging their sense of the truth into a temporary *doze*, they should *make believe*, that they knew no better! As if the God of Truth and Father of all lights resembled an Oriental or African Despot, whose courtiers, even those whom he had himself enriched and placed in the highest rank, are commanded to approach him only in beggars' rags and with a beggarly whine.

I on the contrary find "the Scripture model of devotion," the prayers and thanksgiving of the Psalmist, and in the main of our own Church Liturgy, perfectly conformable to the highest and clearest convictions of my *Reason*. (I use the word in its most comprehensive sense, as comprising both the *practical* and the intellective, not only as the Light but likewise as the Life which *is* the Light of Man. John i. 4.) [11] And I do not hesitate to attribute the contrary persuasion principally to the three following oversights. First (and this is the Queen Bee in the Hive of error), the identification of the universal Reason with each man's individual Understanding, subjects not only different but diverse, not only *allo*geneous but *hetero*geneous.

Second, the substitution of the idea of the Infinite for that of the Absolute. Third and lastly, the habit of using the former as a sort of Superlative Synonime of the vast or indefinitely great. Now the practical difference between my scheme and that of the Essayist, for whose talents and intentions I feel sincere respect, may perhaps be stated thus.

The essayist would bring down his understanding to his Religion: I would raise up my understanding to my reason, and find my Religion in the focus resulting from their convergence. We both alike use the same penitential, deprecative and petitionary prayers; I in the full assurance of their congruity with my Reason, he in a factitious oblivion of their being the contrary.

The name of the Author of the Natural History of Enthusiasm is unknown to me and unconjectured.[12] It is evidently the work of a mind at once observant and meditative. And should these notes meet the Author's eye, let him be assured that I willingly give to his genius that respect which his intentions without it would secure for him, in the breast of every good man. But in the present state of things, infidelity having fallen into disrepute, even on the score of intellect, yet the obligation to shew a *reason* for our faith having become more generally recognized, as reading and the taste for serious conversation have increased, there is a large class of my countrymen disposed to receive, with especial favour, any opinions that will enable them to make a compromise between their new knowledge and their old belief. And with these men, the author's evident abilities will probably render the work a high authority. Now it is the very purpose of my life to impress the contrary sentiments. Hence these notes.

S. T. COLERIDGE.

1. The Greek is ungrammatical (it should be 'houtos cosmos') for euphony's sake, explains H.N.C.
2. Iamblichus (died *c.* A.D. 330), Syrian neo-platonist and mystic, author of a life of Pythagoras quoted below.
3. 'Living words'; see *AR*, p. vii, where Coleridge suggests that

Horne Tooke's *Ἔπεα Πτερέοντα*, or *Winged Words*, would be better named *Λόγοι Ζώοντες* ('living words').

4. *Symposium*, 203a.

5. Iamblichus, *Life of Pythagoras*, 146, much altered.

6. Published anonymously, London 1829, but in fact by Isaac Taylor (1787–1865), artist, writer, inventor, and lay theologian.

7. Borrowed from F. H. Jacobi, *Ueber eine Weissagung Lichtenbergs*, in *Werke* (Leipzig, 1816), III (1816), p. 211.

8. This is probably a distillation of the discussion of Being in *De Trinitate*; see e.g. XII. i. 2.

9. Followers of a system of mystical Jewish philosophy—but here Coleridge refers to the fifteenth- and sixteenth-century Christian 'cabalists', including Paracelsus.

10. Dionysius the Areopagite, converted by Paul at Athens (Acts xvii. 34), was formerly thought to have written a number of mystical texts (in fact by another 'Dionysius'), in which neoplatonism and Christianity are brought together.

11. John i. 3, all editions, mistakenly.

12. See above, note 6.

APPENDIX.

(*Referred to in page* 100)

My Dear ———,

        In emptying a drawer of under-stockings,[1] rose-leaf bags, old (but, too many of them) unopened letters, and paper scraps, or brain fritters, I had my attention directed to a sere and ragged half-sheet by a gust of wind, which had separated it from its companions, and whisked it out of the window into the garden.—Not that I went after it. I have too much respect for the numerous tribe, to which it belonged, to lay any restraint on their movements, or to put the Vagrant Act in force against them. But it so chanced that some after-breeze had stuck it on a standard rose-tree, and there I found it, as I was pacing my evening walk alongside the lower ivy-wall, the bristled runners from which threaten to entrap the top branch of the cherry tree in our neighbour's kitchen garden. I had been meditating a letter to you, and as I ran my eye over this fly-away tag-rag and bob-tail, and bethought me that it was a bye-blow of my own, I felt a sort of fatherly remorse, and yearning towards it, and exclaimed—'If I had a frank for ———, this should help to make up the ounce.' It was far too decrepit to travel per se—besides that the seal would have looked like a single pin on a beggar's coat of tatters—and yet one does not like to be stopt in a kind feeling, which my conscience interpreted as a sort of promise to the said scrap, and therefore, (frank or no frank), I will transcribe it. *A dog's leaf at the top worn off, which must have contained I presume, the syllable* Ve

—————————————Rily, quoth Demosius [2] of Toutos-cosmos, Gentleman, to Mystes the Allocosmite, thou seemest to me like an out-of-door's patient of St. Luke's [3] wandering about in the rain without cap, hat, or bonnet, poring on the elevation of a palace, not the House that Jack built, but the House that is to be built for Jack, in the suburbs of the City, which his cousin-german, the lynx-eyed Dr. Gruithuisen has lately discovered in the moon.[4] But through a foolish kindness for that Phyz of thine, which whilome belonged to an old school-fellow of the same name with thee, I would get thee shipped off under the Alien Act, as a Non Ens, or Pre-existent of the other World to come!—To whom Mystes retorted— Verily, Friend Demos, thou art too fantastic for a genuine Toutoscosmos man! and it needs only a fit of dyspepsy, or a cross in love to make an Heterocosmite of thee; this same Heteroscosmos being in fact the endless shadow which the Toutoscosmos casts at sun-set! But not to alarm or affront thee, as if I insinuated that thou wert in danger of becoming an Allocosmite, I let the whole of thy courteous address to me pass without comment or objection, save only the two concluding monosyllables and the preposition (Pre) which anticipates them. The world in which I exist is another world indeed, but not to come. It is as present as (if *that* be at all) the magnetic planet, of which, according to the Astronomer HALLEY, the visible globe, that we inverminate, is the case or travelling-trunk [5]—a neat little world where light still exists *in statu perfuso*,[6] as on the third day of the Creation, before it was polarised into outward and inward, *i.e.* while light and life were one and the same, NEITHER existing *formally*, yet BOTH *eminenter*:[7] and when herb, flower, and forest, rose as a vision, in proprio lucido,[8] the ancestor and unseen yesterday of the sun and moon. Now, whether there really is such an elysian *mundus mundulus*[9] incased in the Macrocosm, or Great World, below the Adamantine Vault that supports the Mother Waters, that support the coating crust of that mundus immundus[10] on which we, and others less scantily furnished from nature's *Leggery*, crawl, delve, and nestle—(or, shall I say The Liceum, οὗ περιεπάτουν οἱ τούτου κόσμου φιλόσοφοι) [11]—the said Dr Halley may, perhaps, by. this time, have ascertained: and to him and the philosophic ghosts, his compeers, I leave it. But that another world is inshrined in the Microcosm I not only believe, but at certain depths of my Being, during the solemner Sabbaths of the Spirit, I have held commune therewith, in the power of that Faith, which is "the substance of the things hoped for," [12] the living stem that will itself expand into the flower, which it now foreshews. How should it not be so, even on grounds of natural reason, and the analogy of inferior life? Is not nature prophetic up the whole vast pyramid of organic being? And in which of her numberless predictions has nature been convicted of a lie? Is not every organ announced by a previous instinct or act? The Larva of the Stag-beetle lies in its Chrysalis like an infant in the coffin of an adult, having left an empty space half the length it occupies— and this space is the exact length of the horn which distinguishes the perfect animal, but which, when it constructed its temporary Sarcophagus, was not yet in existence. Do not the eyes, ears, lungs of the unborn babe, give notice and furnish proof of a transuterine, visible, audible atmospheric world? We have eyes, ears, touch, taste, smell; and have we not an answering world of shapes, colours, sounds, and sapid and odorous bodies? But likewise—alas for the man for whom the one has not the same evidence of fact as the other—the Creator has given us spiritual senses, and sense-organs—ideas I mean—the idea of the good, the idea of the beautiful, ideas of eternity, immortality, freedom, and of that which contemplated relatively to WILL is Holiness, in relation to LIFE is Bliss. And must not these too infer the existence of a world correspondent to them? There is a Light, said the Hebrew Sage, compared with which the Glory of the Sun is but a cloudy veil: [13] and is it an ignis fatuus given to mock us and lead us astray? And from a yet higher authority we know, that it is a light that lighteth every man that cometh into the world. And are there no objects to reflect it? Or must we seek its analogon in the light of the glow-worm, that simply serves to distinguish one reptile from all the rest, and lighting, inch by inch, its mazy path through weeds and grass, leaves all else before, and behind, and around it in darkness? No! Another and answerable world there is; and if any man discern it not, let him not, whether sincerely or in contemptuous irony, pretend a defect of faculty as the cause. The sense, the light, and the conformed objects are all there and for all men. The difference between man and man in relation thereto, results from no difference in their several gifts and powers of *intellect*, but in the will. As certainly as the individual is a man, so certainly *should* this other world be present to him: yea, it is his proper home. But he is an absentee and *chooses* to live abroad. His freedom and whatever else he possesses which the dog and the ape do not possess, yea, the whole revenue of his humanity, is derived from this—but with the Irish Land-owner in the Theatres, Gaming-houses, and Maitresseries of Paris, so with *him*. He is a voluntary ABSENTEE! I repeat it again and again—the cause is altogether in the WILL: and the defect of intellectual power, and "the having no turn or taste for subjects of this sort," are effects and consequences of the alienation of the WILL—*i.e.* of the man himself. There may be a defect, but there was not a deficiency, of the intellect. I appeal to facts for the proof. Take the science of Political Economy—no two Professors understand each other—and often have I been present where the subject has been discussed in a room full of merchants and manufacturers, sensible and well-informed men: and the conversation has ended in a confession, that the matter was beyond their comprehension. And yet the science professes to give light on Rents, Taxes, Income, Capital, the Principles of Trade, Commerce, Agriculture, on Wealth, and the ways of acquiring and increasing it, in short on all that most passionately excites and interests the Toutoscosmos men. But it was avowed, that to arrive at any understanding of these matters requires a mind gigantic in its comprehension, and microscopic in its accuracy of detail. Now compare this with the effect produced on promiscuous crowds by a Whitfield, or a Wesley—or rather compare with it the shaking of every leaf of the vast forest to the first blast of Luther's trumpet. Was it only of the world to come that Luther and his compeers preached? Turn to Luther's table talk, and see if the larger part be not of that other world which now is, and without the being and working of which the world to come would be either as unintelligible as Abracadabra, or a mere reflection and elongation of the world of sense—Jack Robinson between two looking-glasses, with a series of Jack Robinsons in secula seculorum.

Well, but what *is* this *new* and yet other world? The Brain of a man that is *out of his senses*? A world fraught "with Castles in the air, well worthy the attention of any gentleman inclined to *idealize* a large property"?

The sneer on that lip, and the arch shine of that eye, Friend Demosius, would almost justify me, though I should answer that question by retorting it in a parody. What, quoth the owlet, peeping out of his ivy-bush at noon, with his blue fringed eye-curtains dropt, what is this LIGHT which is said to exist together with this *warmth*, we feel, and yet is something else? But I read likewise in that same face, as if thou wert beginning to prepare that question, a sort of mis-giving from within, as if thou wert more positive than sure that the reply, with which you would accommodate me, is as wise, as it is witty. Therefore, though I cannot answer your question, I will give you a hint how you may answer it for yourself.—1st. Learn the art and acquire the habit of contemplating things abstractedly from their *relations*. I will explain myself by an instance. Suppose a body floating at a certain height in the air, and receiving the light so equally on all sides as not to occasion the eye to conjecture any solid contents. And now let six or seven persons see it at different distances and from different points of view. For A it will be a square! for B a triangle; for C two right-angled triangles attached to each other; for D two un-equal triangles; for E it will be a triangle with a Trapezium hung on to it; for F it will be a square with a cross in it ⊠ ; for G it will be an oblong quadrangle with three triangles in it ⊡ ; and for H three unequal triangles.

Now it is evident that neither of all these is the figure itself, (which in this instance is a four-sided pyramid), but the contingent *relations* of the figure. Now transfer this from Geometry to the subjects of the real (*i.e.* not merely formal or abstract) sciences—to substances and bodies, the materia subjecta of the Chemist, Physiologist and Naturalist, and you will gradually (that is, if you choose and sincerely *will* it) acquire the power and the disposition of contemplating your own imaginations, wants, appetites, passions, opinions, &c., on the same principles, and distinguish that, which alone is and abides, from the accidental and impermanent relations arising out of its co-existence with other things or beings.

My second rule or maxim requires its prolegomena. In the several classes and orders that mark the scale of organic nature, from the plant to the highest order of animals, each higher implies a lower, as the condition of its actual *existence*—and the same position holds good equally of the vital and organic powers. Thus, without the first power, that of growth, or what Bichat [14] and others name the vegetive life, or productivity, the second power, that of totality [15] and locomotion (commonly but most infelicitously called irritability), could not exist—*i.e. manifest* its being. Productivity is the necessary antecedent of irritability, and in like manner, irritability of sensibility. But it is no less true, that in the *idea* of each power the lower derives its *intelligibility* from the higher: and the highest must be presumed to inhere latently or potentially in the lowest, or this latter will be wholly unintelligible, inconceivable—you can have *no conception* of it. Thus in sensibility we see a power that n every instant *goes out* of itself, and in the same instant retracts and falls back on itself: which the great fountains of pure Mathesis, the Pythagorean and Platonic Geometricians, illustrated in the production, or self-evolution, of the point into the circle. Imagine the going-forth and the retraction as two successive acts, the result would be an infinity of angles, a growth of zig-zag. In order to the imaginability of a circular line, the extröitive and the retröitive must co-exist in one and the same act and moment, the curve line being the product. Now what is *ideally* true in the generations or productive acts of the intuitive faculty (of the *pure* sense, I mean, or Inward Vision—the *reine Anschauung* of the German Philosophers) [16] must be assumed as truth of fact in all living growth, or wherein would the growth of a plant differ from a chrystal? The latter is formed wholly by apposition ab extra: in the former the movement ab extra is, in order of thought, consequent on, and yet coinstantaneous with, the movement ab intra. Thus, the *specific* character of Sensibility, the highest of the three powers, is found to be the *general* character of Life, and supplies the only way of *conceiving*, supplies the only insight into the *possibility* of, the first and lowest power. And yet even thus, growth taken as separate from and exclusive of sensibility, would be unintelligible, nay, contradictory. For it would be an act of the life, or productive *form* (vide Aids to Reflection, p. 68.) of the plant, having the life itself as its *source*, (since it is a going forth from the life), and likewise having the life itself as its *object*, for in the same instant it is *retracted*: and yet the product (*i.e.* the plant) exists not for *itself*, by the hypothesis that has excluded sensibility. For all sensibility is a self-finding; whence the German word for sensation or feeling is Empfindung, *i.e.* an *inward finding*. *Therefore* sensibility cannot be excluded: and as it does not exist *actually*, it must be involved *potentially*. Life does not yet manifest itself in its highest *dignity*, as a self-*finding*; but in an evident tendency thereto, or a self-*seeking*—and this has two epochs, or intensities. Potential sensibility in its first epoch, or lowest intensity, appears as growth: in its second epoch, it shews itself as irritability, or vital instinct. In both, however, the sensibility must have pre-existed, (or rather pre-inhered) though as latent: or how could the irritability have been evolved out of the growth? (*ex. gr.* in the stamina of the plant during the act of impregnating the germen). Or the sensibility out of the irritability? (*ex. gr.* in the first appearance of nerves and nervous bulbs, in the lower orders of the insect realm.) But, indeed, evolution as contra-distinguished from *apposition*, or superinduction *ab aliunde*, is implied in the conception of *life*: and is that which essentially differences a living fibre from a thread of Asbestos, the Floscule or any other of the moving fairy shapes of animalcular life from the frost-plumes on a window pane.

Again: what has been said of the lowest power of life relatively to its highest power—growth to sensibility, the plant to the animal—applies equally to *life* itself relatively to *mind*. Without the latter the former would be unintelligible, and the idea would contradict itself. If there had been no self-*retaining* power, a self-finding would be a perpetual self-*losing*. Divide a second into a thousand, or if you please, a million of parts, yet if there be an absolute chasm separating one moment of self-finding from another, the chasm of a millionth of a second would be equal to all time. A being that existed for itself only in moments, each infinitely small and yet absolutely divided from the preceding and following, would not exist *for itself* at all. And if all beings were the same, or yet lower, it could not be said to *exist* in any sense, any more than *light* would exist as *light*, if there were no eyes or visual power: and the whole conception would break up into contradictory positions—an intestine conflict more destructive than even that between the two cats, where one tail alone is said to have survived the battle. The conflicting factors of our conception would eat each other up, tails and all. *Ergo*: the mind, as a self-retaining power, is no less indispensable to the intelligibility of life as a self-finding power, than a self-finding power, *i.e.* sensibility, to a self-seeking power, *i.e.* growth. Again: a self-retaining mind—*i.e.* memory, which is the primary sense of mind, and the common people in several of our provinces still use the word in this sense)—a self-*re*taining power supposes a self-*con*taining power, a self-conscious being. And this is the definition of *mind* in its proper and distinctive sense, a subject that is its own object—or where A contem*plant* is one and the same subject with A contem*plated*. Lastly, (that I may complete the ascent of powers for my own satisfaction, and not as expecting, or in the present habit of your thoughts even wishing you to follow me to a height, dizzy for the strongest spirit, it being the apex of all human, perhaps of angelic knowledge to know, that *it must be*: since absolute *ultimates* can only be seen by a light thrown backward from the Penultimate,— John's Gosp. i. 18.) Lastly, I say, the self-*containing* power supposes a self-*causing* power. *Causa sui*, αἰτία ὑπερούσιος.[17] Here alone we find a problem which in its very statement contains its own solution—the one self-solving power, beyond which no question *is possible*. Yet short of this we dare not rest; for even the ʿΟ ″ΩN, the Supreme *Being*, if it were contemplated abstractly from the Absolute WILL, whose essence it is to be causitive of *all* Being, would sink into a Spinozistic Deity. That this is not evident to us arises from the false notion, of Reason (ʿΟ Λόγος) as a quality, property, or faculty of the Real: whereas reason *is* the supreme reality, the only true *being* in all things visible and invisible! the Pleroma,[18] in whom alone God loveth the world! Even in man *will* is deeper than *mind*: for mind does not cease to be *mind* by having an antecedent; but Will is either the first (τὸ ἀεὶ πρόπρωτον, τὸ nunquam *positum*, semper *sup* ponendum)[19] or it is not WILL at all.

And now, friend! for the practical rules [20] which I promised, or the means by which you may *educate* in yourself that state of mind which is most favourable to a true knowledge of both the worlds that *now are*, and to a right faith in the *world to come*.

I. Remember, that whatever *is*, *lives*. A thing absolutely life-less is inconceivable, except as a thought, image, or fancy, in some other being.

II. In every living form, the conditions of its *existence* are to be sought for in that which is *below* it; the grounds of its *intelligibility* in that which is *above* it.

III. Accustom your mind to distinguish the relations of things from the things themselves. Think often of the latter, independent of the former, in order that you may never think of the former apart from the latter, *i.e.* mistake mere relations for true and enduring realities: and with regard to *these* seek the solution of each in some higher reality. The contrary process leads demonstrably to Atheism, and though you may not get quite so far, it is not well to be seen travelling on the road with your face towards it.

I might add a fourth rule: Learn to distinguish permanent from accidental relations. But I am willing that you should for a time take permanent *relations* as real things—confident that you will soon feel the necessity of reducing what you now call *things* into relations, which immediately arising out of a somewhat else may properly be contemplated as the *products* of that somewhat *else*, and as the means by which its existence is made known to you. But known as what? not as a *product*: for it is the somewhat *else*, to which the product stands in the same relation as the words, you are now hearing, bear to my living soul. But if not as products, then as productive *powers*: and the result will be that what you have hitherto called *things* will be regarded as only more or less permanent *relations* of things, having their derivative reality greater or less in proportion as they are regular or accidental relations; determined by the pre-established fitness of the true thing to the organ and faculty of the percipient, or resulting from some defect or anomaly in the latter.

With these convictions matured into a habit of mind, the man no longer seeks, or believes himself to find, true reality except in the *powers* of nature; which living and actuating POWERS are made known to him, and their *kinds* determined, and their *forces* measured, by their proper products. In other words, he thinks of the products in reference to the productive *powers*, τοῖς ὄντως ὑπάρχουσιν Ἀριθμοῖς ἢ Δυνάμεσι, ὡς ταῖς προμαθεστάταις ἀρχαῖς τοῦ παντὸς οὐρανοῦ καὶ γῆς,[21] and thus gives to the former (to the *products*, I mean) a true reality, a life, a beauty,, and a physiognomic expression. For *him* they are the ΕΠΕΑ Ζ᾿ΩΟΝΤΑ, ἡ ὁμιλία καὶ ἡ διάλεκτος Θεοῖς πρὸς Ἀνθρώπους. The Allokosmite, therefore (though he does not bark at the image in the glass, because he knows what it is), possesses the same world with the Toutoscosmites; and has, besides, in *present* possession *another* and *better* world, to which he can transport himself by a swifter vehicle than Fortunatus's Wishing Cap.[22]

Finally, what is Reason? You have often asked me; and this is my answer;

> "Whene'er the mist, that stands 'twixt God and thee
> Defecates to a pure transparency,
> That intercepts no light and adds no stain—
> There Reason is, and there begins her reign!"[23]

But, alas!

> ──────"tu stesso ti fai grosso
> Col falso immaginar, si che non vedi
> Ciò che vedresti, se l'avessi scosso."
>
> <div align="right">DANTE, <i>Paradiso, Canto I</i>.[24]</div>

FINIS.

1. 'under-stockings', omitted in third edition.
2. i.e., 'belonging to the people', 'public'.
3. Not patients of the doctor-evangelist, but of St Luke's Hospital for Lunatics, in London.
4. Dr Franz von Paula Gruithuisen (1774–1852), German geophysicist and astronomer, who claimed to have seen evidence of habitation on the moon, a discovery which attracted much contemporary interest.
5. See 'An Account of the Course of the Change of the Variation of the Magnetic Needle,' in *Philosophical Transactions of the Royal Society*, 1692.
6. A difficult phrase: the idea is that everything was steeped in light, rather than illuminated by light from an external source.
7. 'In scholastic theology God is said to possess the excellences of human character not formally (i.e., according to their definition, which implies creature-limitation), but eminently (L. *eminenter*), i.e., in a higher sense.' (O.E.D.).
8. 'in its own light'.
9. 'a neat little world'.
10. 'a filthy world'.
11. Liceum is properly Lyceum, the school where Aristotle and the Peripatetics taught, but here a pun is intended. The Greek means 'which the philosophers of this world peripatized'.
12. Hebrews ii. 1.
13. See Hyman Hurwitz, *Hebrew Tales* (London, 1826), pp. 84–5. Hurwitz was a friend of Coleridge, and included some of his translations in this selection of rabbinical tales.
14. Marie-François-Xavier Bichat (1771–1802), French anatomist.
15. 'totality', 3rd edition; 'total', 1st and 2nd editions, certainly incorrect.
16. 'pure [in the sense of intuitive] vision'.
17. 'a supersubstantial cause'; ὑπερούσιος is used chiefly by Proclus, with much of whose theological writing Coleridge was familiar.

18. 'Fullness'; 'plenitude': see Colossians ii. 9.
19. 'that which is always before the first'; 'that which is never *posited*, but always *sup*-posed'.
20. For these first two rules, cf. the passage from Giordano Bruno's *De la Causa*, quoted by Jacobi in *Werke* (Leipzig), IV(2), p. 17.
21. For translation of and reference to this and the Greek phrases following, see above pp. 145–6, and p. 151, notes 4 and 5.
22. Fortunatus, a hero of medieval legend, stole a wishing-cap from the sultan of Cairo, which transported him instantly wherever he wished to go.
23. These lines are Coleridge's own.
24. Lines 88–90. 'With false imagination thou thyself/Mak'st dull, so that thou see'st not the thing/Which thou had'st seen, had that been shaken off' (tr. Cary).

INDEX.